THIS TIMELY BOOK BRINGS together seven clinical and cultural perspectives on Jungian analysis with children and adolescents. Using the frame of "participant observer", edi─ ─ ─ ─ opens for readers a door onto the ma shadow, cultural complexes, and "othe

The authors in this fine collection exp traditions and histories affect their practices with children and adolescents. Virtually any child and adolescent psychotherapist or analyst will find this book refreshing, engaging, and speaking to both the spirit and troubles of our current times.

—**Robert Tyminski**, DMH

Jungian Adult and Child & Adolescent Analyst (IAAP), author of *The Psychological Effects of Immigrating: A Depth Psychological Perspective on Relocating to a New Place*

---

THE AUTHORS HAVE DONE a remarkable job in presenting their work as Jungian child and adolescent analysts and psychotherapists within diverse cultural contexts. This book provides a unique view of the impact of culture and cultural complexes upon individual development and analytical treatment in a number of different countries and is the first book of its kind in the Jungian child and adolescent world. The contributions from a broad range of gifted international Jungian analysts and psychotherapists are deeply moving and engaging, and essential reading for those who work with infants, children, and adolescents from different cultural backgrounds. It is an inspiring book for all those who are interested in Jungian child and adolescent analysis, as it combines detailed clinical descriptions along with a depth of theoretical insight integrating the work of Neumann, Fordham, and contemporary Jungian child and adolescent analysts.

—**Brian Feldman**, Ph.D.

Child, Adolescent and Adult Jungian Analyst; infant observation seminar leader, past Chief Psychologist Child Psychiatry, Stanford University Medical Center, Visiting Professor in Russia, China, and Senegal

# JUNGIAN CHILD ANALYSIS

*Cultural Perspectives*

Group discounts are available (10 or more copies). Contact dyane_
sherwood_press@icloud.com

Book Design: Dyane Neilson Sherwood
Published in 2022

Analytical Psychology Press
280 Elm Street, Oberlin, OH 44074-1504, United States
https://analyticalpsychologypress.com

ISBN: 978-1-958263-00-6

Library of Congress Control Number: LCCN 2022941324

# JUNGIAN CHILD ANALYSIS

*Cultural Perspectives*

EDITED BY AUDREY PUNNETT

## PREVIOUS WORKS

Punnett, A. (2014). *The Orphan: A Journey to Wholeness.* Sheridan, WY: Fisher King Press.

Punnett, A. (Ed.)(2018). *Jungian Child Analysis.* Sheridan, WY: Fisher King Press.

*In Memory of Gisela Broche and Mario Jacoby*

*And for their love of the child*

# CONTENTS

## List of Figures and Illustrations

# Introduction

## *Audrey Punnett*

There is something very particular in the nations.[1]

It [the nation] is a personified concept that corresponds in reality only to a specific nuance of the individual psyche... nothing but an inborn character, and this may be a handicap or an advantage.[2]

—C.G. JUNG

SINCE THE PUBLICATION OF *Jungian Child Analysis* (2018), I have been contemplating what it means to consider the child or adolescent's heritage, based on their culture and country of origin. Jung knew there is something unique to each culture and country, be this an advantage or disadvantage to our individual psyche. I wanted to understand more about what those unique effects might be. Thus began my quest to find child analysts working in countries around the world to contribute a chapter describing their culture and its history, the family within this culture, and a case study demonstrating how one works therapeutically, given one's own and the child's or adolescent's national culture and the culture of their family. Each analyst would be describing deeply how the cultural complex and the culture of the family would be seen and understood in their work.

Jungian analysts from seven countries around the globe have come together to share their perspectives. The countries represented are Italy,

---

[1] C.G. Jung, Conversations with Carl Jung and Reactions from Ernest Jones, 61.

[2] C.G. Jung, The Swiss line in the European Spectrum, *Civilization in Transition*, CW 10, ¶ 921.

Israel (urban perspective and Kibbutz perspective), Taiwan, Romania, the United States, Brazil, and Russia. My wish is to consider what importance understanding national history and family culture may have for the analysis as we learn more from these authors about what it means to the children and adolescents they work with to belong to their nation. In addition, each author gives insights into how their own cultural heritage affects their work. Not only do these insights apply to children and adolescents, but also to the adults with whom we work, both those who share our cultural background as well as those who come from a different background. These insights may be especially helpful in understanding the shadow elements in our own and other cultures.

Through these chapters, we come to know people who share a common cultural system and how they shape the physical and social world around them and are then shaped by these ideas, behaviors and physical environments.[3] What are the cultural definitions and knowledge people use to live their lives and the ways in which they do so? One of the research methods employed in cultural anthropology is "participant observation," living and participating within a community and gaining a deep understanding of the cultural system by active first-hand experience and participation in daily life.

Although I did not anticipate this before moving to Switzerland for my analytic training, I was to become a "participant observer" during my years there. While there, I saw patients primarily within the English-speaking expatriate community, but occasionally I worked with a Swiss child and family. These Swiss children and families became my informants about their culture. At first, I noticed differences between their culture and mine. For example, Swiss children came home from school for lunch every day, which meant a caregiver, usually the mother, needed to be home to prepare the meal. I noticed that most families took their vacations during traditional vacation times each year. I had to consider that while school lunchtimes and vacations were not organized this way

---

[3] W, Handwerker, *The Construct Validity of Cultures: Cultural Diversity, Culture Theory, and a Method for Ethnography.*

in the United States, they were organized this way in Switzerland and in Switzerland, these ways were considered "normal."

As I learned about these differences, I began to view my own country in a different way. I realized the way raising children was done in the United States was not the only way and maybe not even the best way. I found myself more open and more flexible about how to raise a child. I realized that the cultural values of these parents were important to consider and reflected the culture of the Swiss, living in a small country surrounded by large, powerful neighbors. In addition, during my training I was encouraged to learn about the shadow of the country of origin of my analysands to understand more deeply what they carried within their heritage. I believe the ideas for this book were being germinated during those years.

Just as I became a participant observer of Swiss culture, the authors in this book are participant observers and also allow us to become participant observers by bringing us into deeper understanding of their countries' histories and evolution of family cultures.

As analysts, they are participant observers within their own culture since every analyst must deeply explore the cultural complexes and family culture their patients bring to the analysis. Even though we may share the same cultural background as our patient and their family, we know that from the moment we meet them, we journey into new territory.

Each of the authors in this book also allows us to become participant observers of the cultural history of their nation and the history and evolution of culture within the family. Each chapter brings us into deeper knowledge of another culture and the struggles the analyst and the family have faced and will face, as members of that culture and how that affects their work.

Understanding the culture of a child or adolescent also enhances our understanding of the shadow, and the "Other" in that culture. When we work with a child from a culture not our own, that child and their family become our expert informants about the culture. We are innocent to their ways of being. Learning about their culture is imperative in working with them. Needless to say, understanding their culture is equally imperative for working with adults. Moreover, staying attuned to the culture of the child enhances our understanding of the intersubjective space between the analyst and child. This attunement brings greater knowledge of ourselves in the process and amplifies what Jung has said about both individuals being "affected" in the relationship.[4]

I experienced in Switzerland what Margaret Mead named: "as the traveler who has been once from home is wiser than he who has never left his own doorstep, so a knowledge of one other culture should sharpen our ability to scrutinize more steadily, to appreciate more lovingly, our own."[5] My hope is that you, too, will be influenced by each of these authors as they take us on heartfelt journeys into their cultures and illustrate the deep impact these cultures have on their work and on themselves.

## REFERENCES

Evans, R. I. *Conversations with Carl Jung and Reactions from Ernest Jones*. Princeton, NJ: D. Van Nostrand Company, Inc., 1964.

Jung, C.G. *The Collected Works, Second Edition*. (Bollingen Series XX; H Read, M. Fordham, & G. Adler, Eds.; R.C.F. Hull, Trans.). Princeton, NJ: Princeton University Press, 1953-1979.

——The Swiss Line in the European Spectrum, *Civilization in Transition, The Collected Works, Vol. 10, Second Edition*. (Bollingen Series XX). Princeton, NJ: Princeton University Press, 1928.

——The Psychology of the Transference, *The Practice of Psychotherapy, The Collected Works, Vol. 16, Second Edition* (Bollingen Series XX). Princeton, NJ: Princeton University Press, 1946.

Handwerker, W. P. *The Construct Validity of Cultures: Cultural Diversity, Culture Theory, and a Method for Ethnography*. American Anthropologist 104, 1, 106-122, 2002.

Mead, M. *Coming of Age in Samoa*. New York, NY: HarperCollins Publisher, 2001.

---

[4] C.G. Jung, The Psychology of the Transference, *The Practice of Psychotherapy*, CW 16, ¶ 375.

[5] M. Mead. *Coming of Age in Samoa*, 2001, 11.

CHAPTER 1

# Analytical Treatment of Children and Adolescents in a Country Fraught with Contradictions and Conflicts

## *Moshe Alon*
Tel Aviv, Israel

## Introduction

It is with an overwhelming sense of awe that I embark on the task of writing a chapter about the analytical treatment of children and adolescents in Israel for this important book on child and adolescent analysis around the globe. This task entails a great deal of responsibility, for I seek to present matters as objectively as possible, yet without in-depth inquiry of work done in this field by others in Israel. Rather, my descriptions are based on my own experience and countless informal discussions with colleagues I held during my more than forty years working with children in Israel. I take the invitation to write this chapter as a worthwhile and serious challenge, both as an opportunity to describe and conceptualize the uniqueness of analytical treatment of children and adolescents in Israel, and an opportunity to help promote this field worldwide. Within the field of psychotherapy, the analysis of children and adolescents from the Jungian perspective is still in its infancy and requires a great deal of thought, conceptualization, and writing. At the first conference held in this field in Moscow (April 2019), the need for further development became apparent, indicating the importance of providing as many different perspectives as possible.

Based on the assumption that the cultural, social, political, and familial backgrounds serve as the basis upon which analytical treatment of children and adolescents takes place, they need to be described beforehand. The uniqueness of the background in a specific country, which influences the nation's collective unconscious, and manifests among other things in folktale and tradition, needs to be taken into account as well. While I attempt to describe the situation in Israel and I am convinced that distinctions between countries surely exist, I am excited about this book and curious whether it will reveal that the shared collective unconscious underlying psychotherapy in all countries ultimately turns out to be the most influential factor.

Over my 43 years as an educational psychologist in the public and private sectors, I have acquired extensive experience in treating children and adolescents, much of it as a Jungian analyst. Over the years, I have personally treated hundreds of children in my clinic, yet most of my knowledge and experience was acquired while I served as the director of the Educational-Psychological Services of the Tel-Aviv-Jaffa Municipality. In this capacity, I was responsible for providing psychological services to the city's schoolchildren from age 3 through the end of high school. I was in charge of educational-psychological services for all educational settings in the city, including special education, individuals and schools in times of distress and wider public emergencies, both within the city and nationwide. As an educational psychologist, my perspective is systems-oriented, and therefore, I indirectly served hundreds of thousands of children in the city of Tel-Aviv-Jaffa, representing diverse strata of Israeli society.

This diversity needs further explanation. Although Israel is a democratic state, in which all citizens are equal under the law, it is first and foremost, the only Jewish people's state. It was established consequent to the horrors of the Holocaust, in order to assure the Jewish people's physical safety. Therefore, the Israeli Defense Force (IDF) is an important factor in assuring this safety, and it becomes a conflicting matter for the non-Jewish citizens, who are torn between their non-Jewish identity and their loyalty to the state of Israel as their homeland. The non-Jews in Israel are about 20% of the overall population, and therefore, they are seen and treated as a minority. Hence, while being a minority is a disadvantage per se, the state of Israel prioritizes the non-Jewish minority by not enforcing mandatory military service of them, and furthermore, they are prioritized in acceptance to public academic programs.

Another minority, whose Jewish identity and citizenship in a democratic state is conflicting, is the pious Jews, referred to as Haredi. Haredi youngsters are not obliged to be drafted, as they can declare themselves as Torah students, an opportunity which is often misused. This exemption creates another conflict area among the Jewish Israelis. As an educational psychologist in a mixed city, I have worked with all minorities as well, and therefore, I believe this broad experience uniquely qualifies me to represent the work of child analytic therapists in Israel.

## Cultural background

Neumann[1] pointed out that the influences of the collective unconscious transmitted to the child through the mother's embeddedness in society and culture, are important components in the development of his or her consciousness from the outset of life. Children in Israel grow up in a country fraught with contradictions and conflicts, a country whose social structure is extremely complex and influenced by its history, myths, geography, and topography as well as by its national security statutes. Israeli society encompasses two national groups, the Jewish majority and the Arab minority, which constitutes 20% of the population. These two groups live together under a great deal of tension and are engaged in an ideological and religious struggle that often spills over into physical violence. The society is also divided into three main religions—Judaism, Islam, and Christianity—and the country is home to the holy sites of all three religions, which makes matters even more sensitive, particularly in Jerusalem. In addition, Israeli society is divided along two ideological axes: a political axis ranging from right to left, and a religious axis ranging from atheism to ultra-Orthodox Judaism.

---

[1] E. Neumann. *The Child: Structure and Dynamics of the Nascent Personality.*

Polarization along these two axes leads to struggles and conflicts, manifesting through media, educational curricula, attitudes toward "others" in the conflict over the question of religious ceremonies and in the very fabric of everyday life. The atheists seek to separate religion and state and allow pluralism, while the ultra-Orthodox factions call for legislation requiring Israel to be a Jewish state. This religious versus secular conflict is one of the most extreme conflicts in Israeli society for it touches upon fundamental decisions critical to the well-being of all citizens, including decisions about school curricula, the opening of businesses and services on the Sabbath, and interpretations of religious laws.

The State of Israel has its gate wide open for Jewish immigrants from around the world which consequently leads to a multi-cultural and multi-lingual society. In some cities, the classroom includes children who speak a variety of languages. In addition to new individual immigrants who adapt and adjust to society, there are also entire communities who live together within Israeli society, such as the community from Ethiopia and that of labor migrants and refugees. Other conflicting groups within Israeli society are between Mizrahi Jews (originally from Arab countries) and Ashkenazim (originally from Europe), between those residing in the center of the country and those near the borders, and those differing by socioeconomic status and level of education.

The long, rich, and anguished history of the Jewish people has a substantial influence on Jewish-Israeli society, amplified by the current and longstanding state of war with the Arab world in general and more recently with the Palestinians in particular. Jewish Holidays and civil memorial days throughout the year are marked by a positive/negative polarity, creating the myth of a nation's individuation journey leading from slavery to freedom, darkness to light, fear of destruction to victory, and Holocaust to redemption.

The most traumatic and thus transformative event in the Jewish history of modern times is the Holocaust—the massacre of the Jews of Europe during the Second World War. This event is fundamental to the Israeli collective unconscious as it manifests in the constant reminder of the annihilation danger threatening the Jewish people throughout history. In addition to the constant reminders of the Holocaust in the Israeli internal dialogue, a very influential aspect of this memory is the youth pilgrimages to Poland and to the extermination camps. The expeditions are open to all juniors in high school and are usually paid for by the parents, although financial aid can be provided. Participation is not mandatory, and therefore, the non-Jewish students are free to choose whether to join and some do. Through this pilgrimage, the juniors are closely exposed to the horror and sights of the Holocaust. As the memory of the Holocaust is actively kept alive in the Israeli narrative, it also revives both the threat of annihilation and the importance of having a homeland for the Jewish people. Thus, any attack on Israel activates this memory.

On the side of threat, a strong such activation took place in the 1973 war, known as Yom Kippur War, when Israel was attacked on the holiest day on the Jewish calendar, Yom Kippur. This war began with a sense of disastrous failure and a concrete threat to survival. However, it ended with a glorious victory for the Israeli troops. The Yom Kippur war became an integral part of the Israeli narrative of the threat of annihilation and destruction and of struggle leading to victory.

Culturally holding these poles of threat and survival implies notable respect given to the victims of the struggles, manifesting in Memorial Day rituals. Respect is given separately (though just one week apart) to the victims of the Holocaust and to all victims who have died in the wars creating and preserving Israel. Both Memorial days begin with a two-minute horn signal, during which all activity ceases. Schools and media devote this day to memorial stories and ceremonies, and as the days are declared as national mourning, all entertainment is shut down. The atmosphere of respecting the victims is strongly embedded in the Israeli collective unconscious and strengthens the myth of heroic battle as the national narrative.

An important manifestation of the rapid transition between the two poles is that Memorial Day was intentionally set on the day before Independence Day to mark the duality of sorrow and joy. In an abrupt transition at 7:00 pm, the pain and grief over the loss of the wars' victims are immediately replaced by joyous celebrations of independence.

An example of a myth from the distant past that demonstrates the endless devotion to the spirit of freedom is the story of the Masada rebellion, which reverberates through the Jewish unconscious in Israel. It is the story of a thousand Jews, who in the year 73 CE on Mt. Masada, which was about to be conquered by the Romans, decided to commit mass suicide rather than fall into enemy hands and become slaves. Today this mountain site is an important destination for school and youth movement trips, as well as for families and tourists, indicating its importance to the Jewish-Israeli narrative.

A myth currently prevalent in Israeli society is that of Israel as a "start-up nation." While this myth encourages creativity, motivation, and promotes success and pride, it also generates anxiety, stress, and feelings of inferiority among those who are not partners in this success. A longstanding myth associated with the Jewish people is related to our identification with being scholars and being the People of the Book based on the following biblical verse: "This book of the law shall not depart out of thy mouth, but thou shalt meditate therein day and night"[2] One expression of this myth is the annual book fair held simultaneously in many cities across Israel. This fair, known as Hebrew Book Week, promotes and sells books from various areas of interest, all written in Hebrew. Lastly, a myth which may also indicate a meaningful projection which originates in the collective unconscious, derives from the verse: "then ye shall be Mine own treasure from among all peoples"[3] This verse implies a demand set by God, or by the Self, to the highest ethical level, inspiring Jews toward goals and actions empowering the individual and society all over the world.

The small geographic area of the State of Israel also encompasses contradictions. Only 210 kilometers separate the snowy and rainy mountainous northern area (reaching 2,236 meters in altitude) from the arid southern region containing the lowest point in the world (the Dead

---

[2] Joshua 1:8.
[3] Exodus 19:5.

Sea, 400 meters below sea level). As of 2020, the population of Israel numbered nine million, sparsely populated in the southern desert region and the northern mountainous region, while densely populated in the areas around Tel-Aviv-Jaffa and Jerusalem. These two major cities are 65 kilometers apart and represent two social extremes: Tel-Aviv-Jaffa is pluralistic, open, and tends toward the left-wing of the political map, while Jerusalem is conservative, nationalist, and on the political right-wing. Moreover, Jerusalem itself is full of contradictions for it is populated by people from two national groups and three religions.

The population density in a small area, as is the case in Israel's two major cities, greatly increases the potential for conflicts. Every such incident is covered by the various national media in Israel, leaving no room for indifference and generating diverse reactions, some of which find expression in the clinic as well. In 1986 during Israel's First Lebanon War, I was treating an adolescent Arab boy who lived in a mixed Jewish-Arab region. His father was Muslim, and his mother was Christian. His teachers (at the Arab high school) confidentially informed me that his mother was a prostitute. Moreover, his community gossiped that his real father was Jewish. The boy was intelligent and very sensitive, curious, and thirsty for knowledge. He was dark-skinned, and this fact added to his exile experience as he was already excluded at school from both Jewish and Arab circles. Both his psyche and his body bore the scars of many of the conflicts in Israel, and he was torn about his national and religious identity. One interesting anecdote that arose during the course of his analysis was related to my Jewish origins. He told me that when Israeli soldiers were wounded in the war in Lebanon there was a surge of joy among the Arab teachers at his school. I wondered whether he told me this anecdote as a means to please me and to indicate that he did not identify with the Arab side in the conflict but rather with the Jewish side? Or perhaps he was asking me to join him in trying to contain the fact that his identity was split? This case exemplifies how the internal Jewish-Arab conflict is influenced by the broader conflict beyond the borders of Israel, in this case, Lebanon. This reality places the citizens of Israel under a sense of constant threat, and therefore serving in the army is mandatory for Jewish eighteen-year-olds (with the aforementioned exception of the Haredi's). The pervasive threat thus, turns into a constant parental fear for the well-being of those children joining and serving in the IDF for over two years.

My clinical experience shows, that when a youngster (both genders) around the ages of 16 or 17 comes to the clinic seeking treatment, although the immediate and declared reason may be issues of his or her motivation at school, relations with parents, or romantic issues, in most cases the analysis will lead to issues surrounding the coming transition to the next stage of life. Mostly, it would be the coming service in the IDF, however if the youngster is a non-Jew, the analysis will lead to issues surrounding the next step in life, at times the conflict about the army service and at other times, doubts about studies.

As analysis continues through the end of high school and the draft, the anticipated transition will also require therapeutic consideration. Among many adolescents, the processes of the draft involve the fear of death or of being wounded, and they become concrete. In such cases, as an analyst, I am called to contain and make space in which the young patient can express his or her fears and get psychologically ready for the draft, and the consequent inevitable separation from school, home, family, and friends. It is important to point out that at the back of the minds of these adolescents awaits another customary rite of passage for the youngsters who served the army, in the form of the Big Trip, following the completion of their service and before their enrollment to procure higher education. This is a custom which most youngsters adopt, and who mostly work hard to save the money for. Usually, the trip has the nature of a backpacking trek over the course of several months to some far-off destination, presumably a reaction to the limited, narrow, and closed period of army service.

Along with the cases of coping and preparing for the draft, the same is true in cases of patients who suffer from terror experiences or were exposed to them through close relatives. In such cases, child therapists often find themselves in the position of needing to boost their patients' self-confidence which was undermined during emergencies. Disregarding these matters in the clinic would be wrong and indeed impossible, for such disregard might be interpreted as fear and anxiety on the part of the therapist to cope with such terrifying and morbid topics.

The various emergency situations Israeli civilians are confronted by activate waves of after-shock and trauma that harm the children's immediate community and find their ways into the educational system. Hence, the state trains consultants and educational psychologists in the skills needed to assist the community with processing traumatic incidents. Every day throughout the year, the task of the educational system is to help students cope emotionally with emergency situations that harm the community, especially those that are harmful to children. In order to assure the children's physical safety, each year one day is devoted to practicing preparedness for an emergency of any type, including using shelters.

Child and adolescent psychotherapy in Israel takes place in this complex environment. I believe that every child therapist or analyst in Israel must be sensitive to this diverse complexity, to the aforementioned dividing lines which are unique to Israeli society, to the myths and unconscious streams within the society and to the events which transcend social and national borders. For if a child therapist fails to do so, he or she is liable to fail at critical junctures in his or her patients' psychological development, their psychic health, and his or her task.

## The Family

For Israelis, family has supreme value. According to both Jewish and Islamic traditions, individuals are encouraged to establish a family and give birth to children. The underlying expectation is well-sensed on the surface. Despite the major rise in the number of same-sex and single-parent families in recent years, the traditional family structure of father, mother, and children is still considered the norm in Israel. Indeed, in Israel, the median age at first marriage is lower than in the rest of the western world, and the Israeli average of more than three children per family is the highest among all OECD nations. Among minority groups in the population such as the Jewish Orthodox and Arab communities, the average number of children approaches five per family. The investment in fertility medicine, including treatments for older and unmarried women, is high and unmatched in the western world.

Consequently, significant importance is given to the various aspects of child-rearing. Both parents and the government invest major resources in education, to the point that Israel's education budget is second only to its defense. However, Israel's education system is thought to be relatively conservative compared to other western nations, and classrooms are often overcrowded. For these reasons and others, many children require individual help and educational and therapeutic intervention. Among other things, this is evident in the fact that a portion of the family budget, for many families, is allocated to private lessons, after school activities, and youth movements. My experience as a child analyst shows that setting a time for a session is often difficult because children are busy with scheduled after-school and evening activities or play dates almost every day, requiring parental scheduling and involvement. In most families, both parents work and are not home during the day, so that other family members are enlisted to help raise the children and manage the logistics of their daily routine.

Families in Israel, along with society, place great importance on nurturing and developing children's social capabilities. From a young age, children are encouraged to make friends and get together after school, arrange play dates, and attend various afterschool sports and other activities. Older children are encouraged at home as well as at school, to take part in youth movement activities, which are quite typical of Israeli society. The importance attributed to social participation also finds expression in the parents' willingness to invest major efforts in choosing the preschool or school their children will attend. They are guided in this choice by the social group to which the children belong or the group to which their parents aspire. In deciding what high school to attend, teenagers are influenced also by social considerations. Children whose social status is good, though their academic achievements are low, suffer less and are considered to be less problematic than their peers with high academic achievement who have difficulty finding their place in the social hierarchy. Children with difficulties in both areas usually have serious emotional problems. Thus, problems in forming social ties and social ostracism are among the most common reasons for seeking psychological treatment for children.

"Helicopter parenting" is an interesting concept that has emerged in Israeli society, to represent typical parenting. The term describes parents closely shepherding their children beginning at an early age and through their army service, hovering over them and supervising from a bird's eye view, while occasionally landing and intervening in their defense, often beyond what is necessary. The term also describes parents who intervene during analysis, whether directly or indirectly, such that the analyst must make major efforts to understand this family dynamic. He or she is asked to be willing to let the parents take some part in the process. Therefore, children in Israel grow up with an underlying message of importance to the traditional family structure and familial ties, a message shared by the analyst, who must also hold in mind the anticipated changes in Western Culture's perception of family.

## Psychological Therapy

Israel is a social welfare state and thus the children's therapeutic space is quite developed and aims to ensure that all children who are in need of aid are detected and diagnosed. The public service structure consists of developmental psychologists specializing in early childhood, alongside a quite advanced educational psychology system, which is attached to and associated with the education system. Nevertheless, as public services which do not entail any financial cost, they are limited in their ability to meet all needs and to provide long-term therapy. Hence, alongside these public services, there is an array of therapeutic options in private settings and clinics, usually paid for by the parents though sometimes funded by public organizations such as welfare services, the Ministry of Defense, the National Insurance Institute, or various associations.

Treating children and adolescents requires maintaining contact with all entities relating to the child--his or her parents, the educational staff, the school counseling staff, and welfare organizations in the community. In my work with children, this role of "case manager" was enabled by my position in the public sector and often proved itself to be crucial to the success of the analysis.

Methods of child therapy in Israel are diverse, ranging from art therapists in the schools to psychological treatments using a variety of therapeutic approaches. The scope of analytical psychology in treating children in Israel is relatively limited and has only recently emerged, along with the general awakening to this topic in the analytical world. However, sandplay therapy, which originated within analytical psychology, although it is no longer limited to this field, has been prevalent in Israel for many years.

A unique venture in the child analysis world was the boarding school of Neve Tse'elim. Up until recently, this boarding school was operated in the spirit of the analytical approach of Erich Neumann and was a unique component of analytical therapy for children in Israel. The director of the center, Marion Baderian, studied under Neumann's supervision and was a prominent Jungian analyst. She established the center in the spirit of his theory and trained the staff accordingly. The physical plant was built to match the analytical atmosphere. Mandala drawings are painted on the bulletin boards and the walls of the dormitories, and a well, situated in the middle of the central yard, symbolizes the Self and serves as a point of connection to the world of the unconscious. Although today the center is no longer under analytical administration, the physical plant remains as it was and hopefully still unconsciously serves the students' psyches.

Describing the analytical work done with children in Israel one should remember that the child analysts themselves are subject to all the aforementioned background influences. These conflicts also make their way into the clinic as a temenos and direct the therapeutic relationship. For example, there have been cases in which a child undergoing analysis in my clinic has grown up in an extreme ultra-Orthodox family, while I am at the other extreme as secular. During analysis, the child may ask questions referring to obvious aspects of the gap between us, such as questions about wearing a skullcap, or do I believe in God. Analysts in Israel must keep their awareness of the presence of personal views and perspectives, perhaps more than analysts in other western countries, in which there are less acute civil conflicts. The tension of existential opposites exists within the transference and countertransference present in every therapeutic session.

Beneath these processes are fears and doubts, at times with the child's parents as well, relating to issues of trust, respect of differences, and the ability to support someone on a path different from one's own. For example, male analysts must be aware of the avoidance of touch of an ultra-Orthodox mother, meaning hands are not shaken, and in addition, sessions set on to religious holidays' dates are subject to cancellation. In certain sectors, these discrepancies find expression in the topics discussed in the session. For instance, in ultra-Orthodox society and Arab society talking about sexual abuse is highly charged and almost incapable of being discussed, whereas in secular society, the issue, charged as it is, is discussed.

Israeli Jewish analysts have at their disposal an additional element in their toolbox —the abundance of Biblical stories and Jewish tales and their interpretations by different streams of Judaism, such as Hassidism. These mythological stories are personified by flesh-and-blood individuals and contain meaningful lessons. James Hillman[4] made use of one to begin his important article titled "Betrayal". He used the Jewish tale of a father who encourages his son to jump down the stairs into his arms, each time from a higher step. Ultimately the father does not catch his son, who falls and is injured. Thus, the loving and loyal father "betrays" his son, to indicate the wound by the loving figure. Hillman moves to elaborate on the seed of betrayal in all primary relationships.

Another archetypal theme Hillman[5] pointed to as important to all therapeutic encounters is death, particularly when it becomes concrete. Although it is not unique to child analysis in Israel, it is of relevance to child analysis as a whole. Death may come into the session concretely when the child experiences a close relative's death, natural as a grandparent's death or unnatural as in the case of an accident or fatal illness of a younger relative. Importantly, death may also appear symbolically, as psychological growth entails a symbolic death of the old phase. Personally,

---

[4] J. Hillman. *Loose Ends.*
[5] J. Hillman. *Suicide and the Soul.*

as I am older and working with children, death often appears in questions relating to my age and health. The following case studies exemplify the themes discussed and indicate ways in which they are interwoven into the therapeutic work.

## David

David (a pseudonym) began analysis when he was 16 years old, a month after his brother committed suicide during his military basic training. His analysis with me lasted five years, took place in my private practice and was funded by the Ministry of Defense.

David grew up in a lightly religious family and his parents divorced when he was eight years old. His two older brothers chose to live with their father, while David's mother fought for David and he remained with her. She worked as a high school teacher while his father made a living in arts management and teaching. Both David's parents were focused on their own careers, almost completely neglecting his needs for care and attention. They failed to find interest in him and were not involved either in his life or in the therapy. My attempts to meet them were unsuccessful, to the point that I ceased to invite them to meet with me.

Although David attended a religiously oriented high school, during his first two years of analysis the issue of religion did not occupy him and seemed to be hardly meaningful. His school performance was average before his brother's tragic death and greatly declined after the suicide. Nevertheless, he made sure to attend, although he hardly devoted any time to study, and did not take exams nor did he pass the matriculation exams at the end of high school. Because David attended school regularly and his social encounters there were important to him, I assumed he unconsciously understood that school had some value as an organizing structure and a framework that kept him from sinking into depression.

The first two years of David's analysis were devoted to processing the loss of his brother, the ways his family coped with it and the fact that it was a suicide. The death of his older brother enabled David to reframe his role in the family, no longer being the youngest among three brothers whose opinion was never taken into account. Indeed, during the first two years of his analysis, David gained strength and began acquiring a more significant role in the family. A year and a half into his analysis, as his recruitment date drew near, David opposed the idea of serving in combat, and with the help of the welfare services in the Ministry of Defense, he was assigned to a military-clerical job in the center of the country and close to home.

At this stage, many therapeutic hours were devoted to preparing David for his separation from his family and home, and to his transition into the army. In our discussions, we talked a great deal about this transformative transition that had been forced upon him as part of the Israeli experience. Among other things, we saw this transition as an opportunity for him to open up to new aspects of Israeli society with which he was unfamiliar, such as the secular population and encounters with the opposite sex.[6] David's military basic training went smoothly, and this initial successful transition was strengthening and ensuring he would be able to cope with the rest of his service. As his brother's suicide was a month into basic training, this was the focus of the therapeutic process as David was naturally flooded with concerns.

In the first month of his analysis, David had a dream—the only one during his analysis. He described,

*Dad came to pick up me and my two brothers from Mom's house. In the dream, Dad lived in the building where he worked, a huge high-tech facility with lots of sophisticated products. That's where he took us. We drove there in a car. We arrived at the building, got out of the car, and didn't know where to enter the building. Then my brother A (the one who suicided), emerged from the side of the building and I saw him and went with him and entered the building. We were in the lobby, I stood near a military position and a hologram of a battlefield appeared. We were on a battlefield with guns. My dead brother and I played at killing each other. I did not manage to kill him.*

Before approaching the dream from the individual level, two

---

[6] In the religious education sector, boys and girls are assigned to separate classes, and even separate schools, from a relatively early age.

prominent motifs from the collective Israeli unconscious are apparent. The first is the battlefield, which is a real-world Israeli reality that serves as a metaphoric image to David's inner world. The second is the high-tech facility, another Israeli motif as a start-up nation, appearing in the dream as his father's home. It is also questionable whether in the dream it can be a representation of excellency, ambitiousness, creativity, rationalism, coldness, and alienation, or any combination of these. Seen from the individual level, the dream may suggest that the father initiates his sons' transition from the matriarchal to the patriarchal[7]. As while still married, the father failed to fulfill his patriarchal role, the question arises whether or not the divorce unconsciously aimed at his fulfilling that role. In addition, as David was forced to live with his mother after the divorce, his development called for this transformative move from the mother to the father. Yet, in the dream, he needed to discover the entrance to the building, which represented masculinity, by himself, for his father provides him no guidance in finding the entrance. Indeed, in the dream, it was the dead brother who showed David how to enter the building, and his entrance entailed engaging in a battle with his brother but not necessarily killing him. That is, David must "find the entrance to his masculinity", and in order to do so, he must battle against the tragic meaning of his brother's suicide. In reality, his brother did not survive this transition as he killed himself during basic training, which represents a point of transition. In the dream, although David was required to fight for the sake of his development, he did not kill, and therefore the dream may be compensatory in the sense that it compensates David's guilt for "killing" his brother by not dealing with the loss and the grief in his real life.

A sense of guilt frequently arose in our conversations, in the form of his doubts about the nature and scope of grieving. The transition from the matriarchate to the patriarchate entails a separation from the mother, and as David's mother fought for him, the dream suggested she may not have supported the transition I believed David was called

---

[7] E. Neumann. *The Child*.

to make. In addition to the universal call for this transition, the Israeli reality of mandatory draft intensifies the separation from the realm of the Mothers to that of the Fathers. As such, it came to my attention that the dream manifests the road map to his "hero's journey", and that I am called to support and possibly even facilitate his journey, being a male analyst, and a representative of the patriarchate world.

After the completion of his basic training, David was assigned to serve in a Tel-Aviv-Jaffa base. For him, being thus far contained within a restricted religious education, this new position in the big secular free city of Tel-Aviv-Jaffa symbolized a rebirth. At first, he faced multiple crises due to his social difficulties and his encounter with the "others"—be they women, seculars, LGBT, or more. As David adjusted to this new phase of his life, his religious convictions became stronger and it seemed that the high-tech facility from his dream was a synagogue. Was this the patriarchal phase that his psyche acknowledged as safe to enter after leaving the matriarchate? It seems that David found refuge in religion, which could heal his psyche. Pursuing religious studies and obeying the commandments served as foundations he urgently needed and filled the void left after his brother's suicide. The rabbi offered guidance David lacked from his parents, the religious laws performed as a behavioral directing structure and the time-consuming religious studies added some meaning to the meaningless sense of the death[8].

As a secular analyst, watching David's growing religious observance was a big surprise. The disparity between our opinions and beliefs was huge, and I had to remain alert to the danger that my personal opinions would surface and be interpreted as a disagreement based on my secular beliefs and lack of religious faith. Particularly due to my secularity, my support in his process was highly important and granted even more validity to his choices and his journey of self-discovery. I served as a father figure by encouraging him to study Torah, yet unlike his father, both in reality and in the dream father figure who does not enter the building, I remained beside him and with him.

---

[8] I. Orbach & M. Iohan, *Pathology and Risk Factors in Suicidal Adolescents.*

During the fourth year of his analysis, David was unexpectedly chosen as one of Israel's 120 outstanding soldiers for that year. This honor entitled him to participate in an impressive ceremony on Independence Day in the presence of the President, the Prime Minister, and the Chief of Staff. This annual event, attended by the soldiers' families, is broadcast live on Israeli television and is considered an honor of the highest distinction. David felt like an anti-hero and undeserving of such an honor, as his self-esteem was low to begin with. That he was not a combatant validated his anti-hero sense of Self. Yet his therapeutic Hero's Journey did serve to gain him recognition as an "outstanding" religious man, an honor that pleased David and that he felt he deserved. Toward the end of David's army service, the analysis prepared him to continue on his path of extremely devout religious studies.

Working with David and witnessing his growth through analysis, enabling his Hero's Journey to become religiously observant as a way of life, was significant for me as a therapist. As I lead a secular lifestyle this analysis challenged me with embracing the contradictions between religiosity and secularism.

### Muhammad

Muhammad (a pseudonym) began analysis at the age of 8 after having been sexually abused by his older brother, and the sessions took place at a mental health clinic in the public sector. Muhammad's family had fled to Israel from the Arab region of the West Bank, as his father's military-security activities for the Israeli side were not well received in his community. The family lived in Israel under the protection of the Ministry of Defense, which also funded Muhammad's analysis.

Finkelhor[9] defined the background for sexual abuse in the family as a situation in which the role and status of the father have been weakened, the family's moral values have been compromised and the family environment is inadequate and lacking in support. All these conditions, and others as well, were present in Muhammad's family.

---

[9] D. Finkelhor. *Child Sexual Abuse.*

Only once, and during our first session, did Muhammad agree to talk, very briefly, about the sexual abuse, and thus, I assumed that the analysis of his damaged body and soul would take time and would be a long and deep journey. At first, Muhammad wanted us to play a board game in which each player follows a spiral path from the margins of the board to its center. While moving forward, the player needs to confront obstacles and devote efforts to gathering forces and means to overcome these obstacles and to reach the target at the center of the board. This game was symbolic of our journey from the outside to Muhammad's inner world. It anticipated obstacles and much resistance, nevertheless hinted that gathering forces will enable reaching the center, that is the Self, which will mean returning to himself after the traumatic dissociation he experienced with the sexual abuse[10].

Later into his analysis, Muhammad preferred games involving shooting darts or baskets. Symbolically, I understood this game as mainly intended to focus my attention on the target of the analysis, telling me it requires an effort, as does shooting into the basket. Although we did not yet directly mention the sexual abuse, it was clear it had influenced Muhammad's psyche in ways that require analytical interventions. Deep into the analysis, when our relationship was strong and stable, and trust was established, the process became close, and retrospectively, it manifested through two stages. First, over several therapeutic sessions, Muhammad said he wanted to sleep, claiming he was "tired." I was extremely anxious about this unusual request, as I understood he tried to reconstruct the abuse scene in which he had slept in the same room with his brother. I symbolically heard the question, "Will you, my analyst, also abuse me after I fall asleep?" Hence, through processes of transference, Muhammad transferred to me his experience of being unprotected and abandoned while sleeping. I also wondered whether the fact that he was an Arab patient and I was a Jewish analyst played a part in the tension and therefore needed to be taken into consideration as well.

After a few sessions of "sleep," analysis reached the heart of the abuse,

---

[10] D. Kalsched. *The Inner World of Trauma.*

and Muhammad wanted to play tickles, a classical request coming from a sexually abused child, which significantly raised the level of my anxiety. This game entailed me lying on a mattress with my eyes closed while he tickled me and then we were to trade places. My first inclination was not to agree to the game, which is ethically forbidden as it entailed physical touch, more so in the case of a boy who had been sexually abused. Yet reluctance to play the game would mean withholding an important analysis opportunity from Muhammad, one that would potentially provide him some relief and bring him back to himself, to the center of his being, to the Self.

I decided to go along with Muhammad's request, assuming his Self was leading us, and he began tickling me. Symbolically, at this phase, he became the attacker while I was the victim. I lay recumbent on the mattress with my eyes closed, my body surrendered to Muhammad's hands, and he could do as he pleased, almost anything, with my body. I was worried he might touch my sexual organs and I would not be able to prevent this beforehand if I was "asleep". As I believe we were directed by his Self, fortunately, this did not happen, and the boundaries were preserved safely so that healing took place. It was amazing to witness how Self-directed Muhammad was, how he came up with a game that reconstructed the sexual abuse he experienced, only this time with him as the abuser. He also had an opportunity to see from the outside, as an observer who imagines what had happened to him. When he was done tickling me, Muhammad had no hesitation suggesting an exchange of roles, so that this time I would tickle him while he lay on the mattress with his eyes closed. This moment of change turned the attacker to a victim and the victim became the attacker. Overwhelmed with anxiety, I began tickling Muhammad as he lay on the mattress with his eyes closed. As I ran my hands over the length of the boy's body not far from his sexual organ, I clearly understood that I was in the position of the attacker. These moments when I touched the vulnerable victim but did not attack or harm him were the most critical moments in the analysis. As an analyst I could not ask for more, despite my profound anxiety that no healing would take place and worse, that this would reconstruct and worsen the abuse, robbing Muhammad of his faith in adults.

After some time in which we played these two games, we arrived at a rehabilitation stage, as Muhammad suggested that we each build a home. A home distinctly symbolizes one's inner home,[11] and therefore in his request, Muhammad was proposing an act of rehabilitation for both of us. His "inner home" had been destroyed as a result of his brother's abuse, and his actual home had been destroyed because his family had been forced to leave their homeland due to his father's activities. In the Arab culture, significant importance rests within the extended family and thus leaving their homeland meant being torn from this important aspect.

In suggesting that I build a home for myself, I believe Muhammad was telling me that as an analyst I also had undergone a transformative journey through the analyst-patient relationship.[12] This is a classic example of the mixture of materials in the alchemical temenos, and demonstrates healing through transference, countertransference, and the "wounded healer". Under this perspective, the analyst absorbs the analyzed material in such a way that he or she becomes aware of the victim and the attacker within himself or herself. The analyzed absorbs the analyst's healing powers, and by doing that, he or she recovers the projection of his or her healing powers, which were thus far projected upon the analyst.[13] [14] Having played the 'building homes' game for a while, Muhammad suggested that we visit each other's "homes" and host each other. This was the climax of the process which brought the analysis to its end.

Shortly before the analysis ended, I was called to a school meeting in order to discuss Muhammad's state. At the meeting, the school staff reported that Muhammad was now a good student, fluent in Hebrew, and happy with bible studies despite his Arab ethnic origins. His social skills

---

[11] A. De Vries. *Elsevier's Dictionary of Symbols and Imagery.*

[12] C.G. Jung. The Psychology of Transference, *The Practice of Psychotherapy,* CW 16. ¶ 353-539.

[13] J. Hall. *Dreams and Transference Countertransference: The Transformative Field.*

[14] D. Sedgwick. *The Wounded Healer.*

were also good and other children sought his company. Overall, I was happy to find that Muhammad was described as a boy with *joie de vivre*.

This analytical encounter brought to my clinic several of the issues I discussed previously, the Jewish-Arab conflict, cultural differences, the role of the parents in minors' analysis, and myself as a case manager.

## Conclusion

A while ago, a journalist randomly approached a Russian analyst at the airport and interviewed her about her recent visit to Israel. The journalist had no idea who her interviewee was, and when the analyst told her she had attended a workshop with her Jungian colleagues in Israel, she asked: "In your therapeutic approach do you believe that if the patient accepts the shadow there is some improvement?" The analyst answered: "It improves the patient's emotional quality of life, and I think that Israel has a special situation in this context. Israel is a dual society. It is polarized between religious and secular people, between Palestinians and Israelis, between left and right. This is a special situation that enables people to work on the duality of the psyche. Even the Torah states that there is a middle course between things, and the Bible contains a great deal of symbolism that refers to this." The journalist continued with her questions: "Do you think this may explain why most people in Israel are emotionally balanced?" The analyst responded: "Perhaps it is incorrect to say that the one who accepts the shadow is better off. It's more accurate to say that this individual is more human. I see this in terms of "Tikkun Olam". "When we take responsibility for our shadow, we are performing "Tikkun Olam."[15]

The concept of Tikkun Olam has been highly valued in Jewish society throughout history. It means that every Jew and the entire Jewish people must take responsibility to help repair the defects of this world, and it seems that the visiting Russian analyst recognized the themes challenging an Israeli Jewish Jungian analyst. The slow and tolerant approach taken

---

[15] L. Elkayam, In Israel There is a Big Jungian Community, We are Meeting and There is a Touch Between Souls. *Haaretz*, 55.

in any Jungian analysis serves as an appropriate therapeutic format for treating children and adolescents in Israel in that the many pressures and events in Israel and Israeli society require time and thorough work to achieve healing.

According to the Happy Planet Index of human well-being for 2019,[16] Israel is ranked 13th in the world, a relatively high ranking and higher than the US, the UK, Germany, and Japan. This high ranking has been consistent for several years now. In view of the aforementioned descriptions of Israeli society as a whole, it is possible that in the final analysis, its resilience, due to its preserved history and myths, is the key which has enabled most families in Israel to cope effectively with the challenges of life in Israel and to feel strong and happy.

[16] *World Happiness Report*, March 20, 2019.

# REFERENCES

De Vries, A. *Elsevier's Dictionary of Symbols and Imagery*. Oxford, UK: Elsevier, 2006.

Elkayam, L. In Israel There is a Big Jungian Community, We are Meeting and There is a Touch Between Souls. *Haartz*, November 22, 2019.

Finkelhor, D. *Child Sexual Abuse: New Theory and Research*. New York, NY: Free Press, 1984

Hall, J. *Dreams and Transference Countertransference: The Transformative Field*. Asheville, NC: Chiron, 31-51, 1984.

Hillman, J. Betrayal. In *Loose Ends*. New York, NY: Spring Publications, 1975.

Hillman, J. *Suicide and the Soul*. Irving, TX: Spring Publications, 1978.

Jung, C.G. *The Collected Works, Second Edition*. (Bollingen Series XX; H Read, M.  Fordham, & G. Adler, Eds.; R.C.F. Hull, Trans.). Princeton, NJ: Princeton University Press, 1953-1979.

——*The Practice of Psychotherapy, Collected Works, Second Edition, Vol. 16*, (Bollingen Series XX). Princeton, NJ: Princeton University Press, 1946.

Kalsched, D. *The Inner World of Trauma: Archetypal Defenses of the Personal Spirit*. New York, NY: Routledge, 2001.

Elkayam, L. In Israel There is a Big Jungian Community, We are Meeting and There is a Touch Between Souls. *Haartz*, November 22, 2019.

Neumann, E. *The Child: Structure and Dynamics of the Nascent of Personality*. London, UK: Karnac Books Ltd, 1973.

Orbach, I. Iohan, M. Pathology and Risk Factors in Suicidal Adolescents. *Journal of Clinical Child and Adolescent Psychology*, 31: 193-205, 1997.

Sedgwick, D. *The Wounded Healer: Countertransference from a Jungian Perspective*. New-York, NY: Routledge, 2000.

*World Happiness Report*. (March 20, 2019). Retrieved from: https://world-happiness.report/ed/2019/changing-world-happiness/

CHAPTER 2

# Child Analysis in Italy:
# Play, Creativity, Individuation

## *Caterina Vezzoli*
### Milan, Italy

## The Italian Culture and Analytical Psychology

I will sketch a short historical background of the origin of Analytical Psychology in Italy and the context of child analysis.

Child analysis in my country was introduced after the Second World War and more specifically in the 1950's. In discussing the beginning of Italian child analysis, I will follow the steps of Mariella Gambino Loriga, one of the pioneers of the new discipline.[1]

In order to understand the development of child analysis we are obliged to speak of Italian culture in the fifties, its connection to the early development of Analytical Psychology and the reality of a nation that after the terrible Second World War had to reconstruct much of its territory, especially in the north, the more developed and industrialized part of Italy.

Ernst Bernhard, a German Jewish exponent of Analytical Psychology, had to flee Berlin in the 1930's. When refused asylum by the British, he opted for Rome. He arrived in Rome in 1937, after having worked with Jung in Zurich in 1936. In Rome he established a collaborative exchange with Edoardo Weiss, the Freudian pioneer in Italy. Together

---

[1] W. Bosio. Mariella Gambino Loriga (1920-2006), Pioniera della psicologia Analitica Infantile l'asilo di Villetta Casana. In *Enkelados, 6,* 97.

they organized a seminar held at the SPI (Società Psicoanalitica Italiana) on "*Introduction to the Studies of Dreams*" (Introduzione allo studio dei sogni). In this seminar on dreams (Seminario sul sogno), Jungian and Freudian analysts worked together.[2] The seminar was published in 1996, 30 years after the death of Bernhard. I'm giving this information to show how, at this time, the psychoanalytic movement in Italy was pervaded by a spirit of reciprocity and exchange.

In 1938 the Fascists' promulgation of racial laws ended their collaboration. In 1939 Weiss fled to the US and Bernhard was arrested and deported to a concentration camp in Calabria. He was imprisoned for about a year and was released through the efforts of Giuseppe Tucci, an Italian scholar of Eastern Religions. Famously, Bernhard dreamt of his liberation by an Italian scholar of Indian religions. From 1941 to June 4, 1944, the day Rome was liberated by the allies, he remained hidden behind walls in his flat in Rome.

As Bernhard resumed his work following liberation, a new culture in Italy, liberated from the oppression of Fascism, was being born. Important figures of the Italian antifascist movement found in Analytical Psychology, and in Bernhard, their way to individuation.[3]

The generation that came of age during the war had known all the devastations, the bombing of the cities, and the suffering produced by the German army after the armistice signed in September 1943 by General Badoglio with the allies. This armistice literally divided Italy in two, with Germans maintaining control in the north. Atrocities and bloodshed there, and in the South, continued until the war ended in May 1945.

This historical background helps to explain the progressive and democratic spirit that inspired Jungian Child Psychology in Italy. After the war Italy had to rebuild, both materially and spiritually. Travel wasn't easy. My first journey to Paris and London was not until 1969 and was by boat and train, as flying was very expensive. In the Europe of the

---

[2] R. Madera. Maestri Scomodi, *Rivista di Psicologia Analitica*, 2, 54.

[3] di Montezemolo, A. Ernst Bernhard e Due Maestri del Cinema Itali. ano: Vittorio De Seta e Federico Fellini. In *Enkelados*, 6, 78.

fifties, travel between Rome and other European countries was especially uncommon for a young woman.

Mariella Gambino Loriga travelled all over Europe during this time to gather information firsthand about the centers that worked analytically with children. Visiting many European countries that were being reconstructed after the destruction of the war was unbelievable for its boldness. I mention her travels because they illustrate the international spirit which animated the first approach to child analysis. I believe the search for international feedback remains a characteristic of child analytical psychologists who are open to the influences of different analytical schools and are interested in doing research in the field.

In addition to these historical and cultural influences, it is important to note that in the first group of analysts around Bernhard, the women were few but important.

Bianca Garufi,[4] an intellectual, analyst and founding member of the first Italian Jungian Society, Associazione Italiana di Psicologia Analitica (AIPA), was encouraged to do her analysis with Bernhard by Bobi Bazlen. Bazlen, an important editorial consultant, was analyzed by Weiss and later by Bernhard. Garufi was a friend of Cesare Pavese, an important antifascist writer, with whom she co-authored a book, (Fuoco Grande), published after Pavese's suicide in 1950. Silvia Rosselli, another early AIPA analyst, was the daughter of one of the Rosselli brothers, important anti-Fascists, who were slain by the Fascists in 1937. Her cousin, Amelia Rosselli, was analyzed by Bernhard. (Some of Bernhard's patients after working with him remained in contact and created a sort of think tank which was very important for Italian culture. Just to give a few names that might be known internationally, Federico Fellini and Vittorio De Seta, two important Italian film directors remained in contact with him. De Seta's films in their neorealism and/or exploration of the interior world remain exemplary in the research of the soul.[5]) Through the analytical process, Amelia Rosselli found her creativity and became a

---

[4] L. Turinese, La Psicologia Oracolare di Bianca Garufi. In *Enkelados, 6,* 49.

[5] A. di Montezemolo. Ernst Bernard e Due Maestri del Cinema Italiano: Vittorio De Seta e Federico Fellini.

poet. Another famous writer who publicly recognized the importance of her Jungian analysis was Natalia Ginzburg, sister-in-law to Adriano Olivetti, discussed below.

These women, important figures in the Italian culture of the fifties and sixties, were pioneers of Italian feminism, women who dared to stand on their own with no inferiority complex towards a culture in many respects unfavorable towards women, especially towards those who dared to speak in public.

## Social Transformation and Children of the Working Class

One of Bernhard's "friends" (a former patient) was Adriano Olivetti, an enlightened businessman who practiced "capitalismo dal volto umano" (capitalism with a human face), which valued the wellbeing and quality of life of his workers as requisites for good work. As part of that quality of life, he believed that the children of women working in his factories should be looked after and taught from kindergarten through elementary school while their parents were working. This was the reason why one morning in February 1956, Mariella Gambino Loriga arrived from Rome, her native town, in Ivrea, a small city in Piedmont, and Olivetti's headquarters. It was Bernhard who suggested her name to Olivetti, even though Bernhard's brief work with Loriga didn't go well. She didn't like his esoteric approach and left the analysis very soon. However, she then worked with Dora Bernhard, his wife, who had worked with Toni Wolff.

Before going to Ivrea, Loriga studied in 1950 at the Davidson Clinic in Edinburgh, run by Winifred Rushforth. In 1951, she studied and trained in Montessori techniques. In 1952, she spent two semesters in Zurich and was in contact with Walter Zublin, a Jungian analyst and child psychiatrist practicing in Bern.

For Loriga, the social transformation of society was extremely important. She believed in an ethical transformation towards equality between classes, between genders and against the elitist supremacy typical of Italian society which had always favored the wealthy over the working class and peasants.

Knowing she was going to Ivrea, she visited Montreux, Lausanne,

Geneva and Zurich to see firsthand the centers that practiced child therapy.

## Children Respected as Instruments
## of Their Own Development

When Loriga arrived in Ivrea, she was supposed to take over a kindergarten for 200 children and 35 workers. It had been organized and run before she arrived by Luciana Nissim Momigliano, a future Freudian analyst who was sent to Auschwitz in 1944 because she was Jewish and a partisan operating in Valle D'Aosta. She survived the concentration camp because she was a doctor, and her work was needed. She left Ivrea and the kindergarten in 1956 with her husband who worked at Olivetti and transferred to Milan where she became a member of Centro Milanese di Psicoanalisi. I'm highlighting these women because independently of their training and background they had the courage and determination to be free of mind, believe in projects that were for the good of future generations but also for a better quality of life in the present. They had the strength and courage to believe in the creation of a better society for everyone, but with special attention to women and children in their care.

In Ivrea, Loriga created Villeta Casana, a new space especially conceived as a house for children. She wanted a simple space where the children could move around, learn through experiences and develop harmoniously. She chose the Montessori method to teach and educate the children.

In the Montessori classroom the children are of mixed ages and the space is prepared so that the children have set areas for practical life, sensorial experiences, mathematics, language and culture. The Montessori method was an important choice because the children could learn through experience, through collaborative play, and through their own creative activities. Montessori-trained teachers offer help by making suggestions to assist the children in their individual process of learning.

Loriga established strong relationships with the children's mothers. She met them during their pregnancy, followed them during their maternity and was well aware that they had a second job as after their work in the factory they had all the household work on their shoulders. The experience put her in contact with the reality of women of all classes and the burden on them from their extended families as well as their immediate family. Loriga was a modern woman in many ways. In the 1950's, in Italy, to be a separated woman, on her own with two children, having a good relationship with her ex-husband and especially with her mother-in-law who came to visit her grandchildren was more suspicious than to be an intellectual. It required great stamina against prejudice, even in the industrial north.

The Olivetti experience lasted until 1960, when Adriano Olivetti died. His firm's policy changed to state support for the children and families.

The experience in Ivrea in the industrial north showed the potential of the work to support the development of children, their mothers and their family. The social responsibility of giving new generations the tools to find, in their own creativity, the possibility to learn and develop themselves was an important step on the road to child analytic understanding and training. The children started to be seen as the instruments of their own recovery with the help of respectful adults who developed with them.

After Ivrea, Loriga decided to live in Milan. She was a founding member of the Milanese section of AIPA. In 1966 she wrote, in collaboration with Mario Trevi, a timely and clear paper on the directions that were emerging in Jungian child psychology. They recognized in Fordham, Neumann, Kalff, and Zublin the trends that were being developed. Her travels throughout Europe to learn how child analytical psychology was practiced and her experiences with children proved to be useful in giving her a clear perception of the lines of development of child analysis. Her concern for children and their psychological well-being paralleled social system emancipation in creating better conditions and good education for the children of what at the time were considered the less-favored social classes.

In this glimpse of the historical background, I wish to emphasize that the women and men who approached Analytical Psychology were animated by a freedom of mind and a desire to create a secular culture far from the prejudices of intellectual superiority and above all from the controlling structures of established power.

After five years of devastating war and twenty years of Fascist oppression, letting the mind wander in what had been forbidden directions helped to recover trust in life, in the future and in oneself. It wasn't only about politics. It was a dream coming true, not only a political program but a desire to create a better world. Many of the avant-garde artists, philosophers and thinkers as well as Jungian analysts were from bourgeois or aristocratic backgrounds, but they asserted their privilege by going beyond their family lineage into a world to be explored and changed.

Mariella Gambino Loriga had the open mind to dare to investigate internationally what the Jungian child scenario had to offer and how this could be integrated or explored in the Italian context. In my opinion the experience Italian analysts obtained outside Italy is the most important aspect of Italian child analysis. Nearby Switzerland, home to Jung and later to the Jung Institute, was a promising land as it offered direct contact with a generation of Jungian analysts who had trained with Jung, and in the 1950's, Jung was still alive. It was a place where many of the early Italian analysts felt drawn to train or at least to visit for some semesters. In the 1970's, the other place important for child analysis was England, as anticipated in the paper written in 1966 by Mario Trevi and Mariella Loriga.

## The Impacts of the Economic Boom and Opposing Political Forces

If the 1950's were the time of reconstruction and utopia, the 1960's were the period of the economic boom. The way of living of the Italian family changed—better salaries, health care, and shorter working days improved the lives of the majority of workers. Free education from kindergarten to university became available in the sixties/seventies. The student movements in 1968 and 1969 with the revolutionary ideology of freedom from conventions and tradition seemed an important moment of openness towards what could become a more equal society. Then came the season of terrorism with subsequent repression and the reemergence of the Fascist movement which never dies, as Umberto Eco teaches us in his book, *Il Fascismo Eterno.*

## Development of the Jungian Societies

After the death of Ernst Bernhard in 1965, AIPA, the Italian Society of Analytical Psychology founded in 1961, home to all Jungian analysts in Italy, split apart and Mario Trevi founded Centro Italiano di Psicologia Analitica (CIPA), the second Jungian Society.

In the 1970's, the two analytical societies became grounded in the Italian Reality. The number of analysts increased and although AIPA was the first to develop a specific training on child psychology, both societies included in their training for adults a course on child analysis. Specific child training was left to each analyst to develop on his or her own. Many of them had clinical experience in children's clinics or hospitals and went to Zurich or to England for periods of time. They also sought supervision and training in other analytic schools. This theoretical openness is what I like most about the child analytic training.

## Personal Lenses in Approaching Child Analysis

I will now speak of the development of child analytic culture in Italy as I lived it and with some of the contradictions, I found in myself and experienced in my development as a child analyst. I did my adult training in Zurich at the end of a long analysis with a founding member of AIPA at the end of which I started to work with children. I chose Zurich because the Italian CIPA and AIPA seemed rather closed, not "revolutionary" enough for my interest. I had spent the end of the sixties and part of the seventies as an activist, first at the University and then in the factory where I worked. When I chose my training after University, the Italian Jungian Societies had lost, to my eyes, the depth and heretical component of renewal that was my preferred aspect of Jungian thought. The Italian training Institutes seemed bureaucratic and limiting of self-creativity. My thinking was of course an idealization of the Swiss training and a denigration of something that I didn't really know; it was a prejudice. I was right, however, in believing that what the Jungian world was producing at the time would be seen and passed through Zurich.

In Kusnacht I could meet the Fordhamian analysts who came to teach, could learn the Neumann theory on child analysis, could follow Dora Kalff in Zollikon and learn how to use fairy tales in analytic work with adults and children. I came to know Miranda Davis's and Mara Sidoli's work with children.

I would discover, on my return to Italy, that perhaps I could have had these experiences in Milan. However, the freedom, the easiness of contact with the "foreigners" that I met in Zurich was far from the formality that I experienced at CIPA in Milan. Zurich made me understand that there wasn't only one way to be an analyst, that the secret to becoming an analyst was in the endless quest to be oneself and to live one's personal myth in modesty.

On my return I started a collaboration with a service for infancy. Following my interests, I continued supervision in Zurich. I had peer discussions with colleagues in Italy as well as group supervision.

At first, I worked as a psychotherapist. For three years, I also conducted research on the dreams of children in an elementary school located in the area where I had my practice. I liked working in the Lombardy countryside even in winter when the fog enveloped the landscape and made my return to Milan difficult. I continued my contact in Zurich for supervision. I worked with the instruments I had mastered during my training and from my experience with the children. I worked with drawings, fairy tales, storytelling, sandplay, mainly playing and observing the children play.

At the beginning, I let my colleague at the infancy service work with the parents. At that time, I didn't think of working with the parents and child, but in time I learned about it. I further developed my understanding and studies of other analytical approaches: Kleinian, Winnicottian, Bionian. In the Jungian field, the Fordham school at the Society for Analytic Psychology (SAP) was an important reference.

## Child Analysis in the Nineties

In 1997, I decided to become part of CIPA. The child analysts there who soon became my friends were those considered less Jungian because they referred primarily to Fordham and to Sidoli. Their approach was mainly clinical. From my point of view as an outsider, I saw their work as very enriching and not in contrast with the classical or archetypal approach. Among the child analysts who worked mainly with a clinical approach was Francesco Bisagni. He had worked with Fordham in London and with Sidoli and also had Kleinian training. His contributions were always very interesting. The other colleagues with similar interests were Rossella Andreoli and Monica Ceccarelli. Adriana Mazzarella, an older colleague whom I remember with affection, supervised me for a short time for sandplay. She was very classical in her approach and an expert on Neumann.

My colleague and dear friend Wilma Bosio, a child analyst with long experience who had worked with Mariella Loriga and Marcella Balconi in Novara, introduced me to the *International Workshop for Analytical Psychology in Childhood and Adolescence*. Immediately I felt at ease and interested in this community of child analysts. In their different theoretical approaches, I had found my world.

The people I met there expanded my analytic world and stimulated my research. I established many lasting relationships. The atmosphere of the workshop was stunning. We worked at the edge of chaos, in the sense that at our yearly meeting we discussed cases and paradoxical theoretical situations apparently without answers. The colleagues very generously opened their hearts and presented themselves unreservedly to the discussion in the small groups. The richness of Analytical Psychology and of the different approaches let emerge the value of not knowing and the dedication of senior and younger analytical psychologists to the work.

## The International Container

At the Workshop the colleagues from Associazione Italiana Psicologia Analitica (AIPA), among them Pierclaudio De Vescovi, Gianni Nagliero and Wanda Grosso, veterans to the meeting, aroused my admiration for their long experience in the treatment of children in private practice and in institutions. Barry Proner's theoretical approach that many defined as Kleinian, surprised me for its depth of analysis and for its understanding of archaic mechanisms. Gustav Bovensiepen remained unsurpassed for his ability to question what seemed to be established theory, never tiring of producing new understanding and new approaches. Brian Feldman's work on infant observation was so enlightening, especially when he presented the influence of different cultural attitudes in the mother/

baby relationship. Maria Teresa Raduan from Brazil could, with only her presence, bring the light and vitality of her culture. My dear friend Brigitte Allain Dupré was always ready to propose another view that further stimulated the discussion, as well as Judith Woodhead, with the kindness and profundity of her approach to parent-infant therapy.

I believe that the international influences on child analysis are vital for all areas of Analytical Psychology. Sidoli's and Bovensiepen's idea to create a group of analysts who could meet every year in an informal way to discuss child analysis demonstrates their trust in the potential of Jungian child analysis and its power of transformation in the analytical world.

## The Family

The Italian family has changed a lot over the years, reflecting changes in Italian society. We went from an extended family background where several generations lived in close contact under the control of the *pater familias*, especially in the countryside and in the south, to the nuclear family where parents and their children lived apart from their extended family, especially in industrial cities and urban areas.

The Family Act of 1975 and later statutes defined relations inside the family and built on changes that had already taken place, including the ratification of the Divorce Law in 1974. The Family Act defined the rights of children-as well as the responsibility of their parents towards them. Today all types of heterosexual families are recognized, including de facto unions.

In those years, Italian state schools were also moving towards a different way of teaching. They never adopted the Montessori method, but respect towards children and their backgrounds slowly increased. Children started to be seen as subjects in their own right. Children from poorer backgrounds had the same benefits as those from more privileged backgrounds, thus, education was granted to children of all social classes.

In the 1970's, Italian primary schools started integrating pupils with disabilities. The quality of teaching for disabled students in the state schools quickly became superior, more respectful and more democratic than that supplied in the private schools, often owned by religious orders.

Another important event of the seventies was what we call "Basaglia's Law" or the "180 law" that in 1978 closed the psychiatric asylums, which were places of torture and maltreatment, and started the treatment of severe psychiatric patients in protected residences and communities more respectful of the humanity of the mentally ill. The "180 law" established the fundamental principle that the mentally ill are not criminals to be imprisoned but patients who need treatment and respect.

In 1978, legal abortion was established as a fundamental right for women, together with the right to sex education and to contraception, confirming the right to a free and conscious sexuality and the right to avoid unwanted pregnancy without risk to one's life.

Italy, a preeminently Catholic country, was moving towards becoming a secular state. Perhaps now, laws would no longer be approved first on the other side of the Tiber (where the Vatican is), but rather by the Italian parliament.

Unfortunately, after the libertarian movements and the laws on parity and equality in the family and in society that marked the sixties and seventies, the 1990's, with the advent to power of Silvio Berlusconi, led to a regression to a vision of superiority of men over women. Berlusconi's numerous television channels feature shows where women are reduced to a vulgar version of scantily clad, mindless young girls, called *Veline*,[6] who parade themselves obeying much older men who are clearly in power. The allusion to a degraded and inferior feminine is evident and has had repercussions on women and on all our society. It is of concern for child analysis because the mothers of children we now work with grew up with the myth of the *Veline*. They often have a confused perception of themselves and suffer from inferiority and that of their children.

In this atmosphere, it is only recently (2016) that LGBT unions have been recognized. Formally the law avoids the word marriage and uses "*unioni civili*" (civil unions). For these couples, adoption of children is not permitted; only one member of the couple can adopt and the procedure is complicated. A court must decide if the adoption, usually

---

[6] *Velina*, (singular) the young girl who moves, winking and provocative. The other meaning is a transparent sheet of paper.

done abroad, can be considered legal. In principle the law grants to all children the right to have a loving family, to be looked after, educated and to have all the assistance they need, however for LGBT families, there is still much to do.

However, fathers and mothers now have equal rights and duties, the "patria postestà" has long been put aside and parental authority can be put into question by the Court in protection of the children.

In Italy, the extended family—grandparents, aunts and uncles, cousins, remain important as affective resources and usually have a role in the upbringing of children. When they live near their grandchildren, grandparents usually have a role in the daily management of children. When the grandparents live far away, the children usually spend time with them during the school holidays in summer and at Christmas. The same is true for the aunts, uncles and cousins. Even following divorce or remarriage, the grandparents often maintain their affective role and a negative aspect of control over the parents and grandchildren. As child analysts in Italy, we have to keep in mind the parents' extended family and understand the explicit and implicit role it plays in the psyche of parents and their children. In cases of divorce and remarriage, the number of grandparents and relatives increases. Relations among all these relatives are not always harmonious.

Usually when respected, the children manage these complicated relationships and disentangle themselves in a more or less practical way: *"Hallo, I want you to meet my brother and sister. They are spending the holidays with me at the grandparents... I mean... my grandparents that you know...!"* The 11-year-old telling me this on the beach in front of my house is very proud to show me his handsome half-brother, 22 years old whom I had never met before and his half-sister, just 20, whom I met on that same beach when she was eight years old. At that time my little friend wasn't born yet; his half-sister is now a beautiful young woman. She doesn't remember me. I look at the three of them on the beach on their paddleboards, swimming like mad and I smile, pleased. I know their father. He worked hard to be present for his older children in a separation and divorce that was problematic for the ex-wife. His older son suffered—being loyal to his mother, he took her side in his wish to protect her. As a result, he refused to see his father, who, for his part, tried in various way to be present and at the same time respectful. The son had to do some therapy to reach a degree of separation from the mother and not feel guilty for his longing for his father. After some years he reached more stability. In time, his mother also attained more stability. The 20-year-old sister grew into a very beautiful and interesting young woman, full of life. She plays her role between her brothers who both tease and love her. My little friend has always loved his siblings and I believe has contributed to create the conditions for a real relationship among them.

During our chats on the beach over the years, he always found a way of speaking of his family which included his half-brother and sister who didn't live with him, although he saw them regularly. The difference in age might have helped the positive relationship. Our "beach" is where he has spent his holidays since he was a baby. He loves it very much, it's his home. It was he who asked his grandparents if he could invite his siblings to visit. They agreed with a sense of satisfaction for the maturity demonstrated by their grandchild. It pleases me to present what can be considered a perfect situation, but in therapy, of course, we see very different things.

## The Parents

When I begin work with a child, I often observe the pressure on the parents. When their children have problems, the parents experience a narcissistic failure. They haven't been able to raise a perfect child. They feel guilty, inadequate, lost. They often compare their children or themselves with others who are more successful because they comply with the standards of the community of reference. Depending on the situation, they try to hide their feelings and abandon their children to a sense of uselessness, or overburden them with anxiety, or create an enemy outside. Italian parents are often very anxious about the performance of their children. The children must show the world that they are intelligent, simpatico, beautiful, sporty. They must be successful, preferably extroverted.

The family is still very important in Italian culture and as child analysts we have to consider it will be present and often demanding in the course of the treatment. For this reason, I try to set clear boundaries. As a child analyst, after the beginning of therapy and once I set the boundaries, I don't see the parents often. If the parents need help, I send them to other colleagues or to a group for parents. Where there are stepparents, I rarely see the new partners of the parents. It is important in my opinion not to undermine the role of the natural parents and to avoid confusion, although exceptions are always possible.

## Analyst, Child, Parents

My relation to the child is exclusive. Metaphorically I leave the family, the school relations, outside the door. I concentrate on the relationship and I try to see the world through the eyes and the experience of my patient. If the child is sent by a school psychologist or professional, I prefer to give information to them instead of speaking directly to the teachers. I have come to this procedure because I value the space with the child as a protected transitional space as well as an experimental space where the child can explore his or her world, to discover his or her resources, to experience the giant emotions that need a secure setting to be contained. A space that can let transitory solutions that might emerge in the course of treatment have their development and eventually be integrated or in due time overcome by more mature ones. In order to let the creativity and the resources operate we need an analytic space with minimum requests for performance to allow the emergence of the unknown. Even with children with limited intellectual resources or with minor cognitive deficits we obtain the best results if we don't pressure them and wait with them for the time necessary to find their way out of the impasse.

When a child is brought for analysis, there is often an implicit request for adaptation to performative tasks that will satisfy a parental need. Parents, teachers or whoever sent the child have the implicit request that we fix the child. We obtain the best outcome when we attune to the child's rhythm and when we can see the world through the eyes of our patient. This requires an empathic attitude allowing the emergence of *the moment of complexity* that will constellate the analytic field. Even if *the moment of complexity* constellates suddenly, time is needed for many reasons. However, in child therapy time is subject to many vicissitudes which do not depend exclusively on the patient-analyst dyad. However, an experience of trust constellated in the dyad can hopefully remain with the child even in the case of abrupt termination.

## In Treatment

Giorgio (pseudonym) was an 11-year-old boy who came to see me after his parents separated because, according to them, he became depressed. His mother called me. She said that Giorgio's father agreed on the need for professional assistance for their son. However, she preferred to come with her son without the father. I didn't understand her request. If the father agreed, why not come together? Kindly I said that maybe this first time I would prefer to see them together if it was tolerable for them.

At the first meeting the three of them enter the office and what surprises me is Giorgio's amazing beauty, so similar to that of his mother, a 35-year-old woman from Latin America, tall, slender, and elegant. The father, a distinguished gentleman in a well-tailored suit, probably Armani, is elderly in appearance, with white hair and a weathered face, probably in his sixties. When they sit down, I introduce myself, using my Christian name to ease Giorgio's tension. I say that in this first meeting we will speak of the reasons that bring them to see me. I add that any of them can start to speak. After a few seconds, Giorgio is the first to break the silence. In those few seconds of silence, the noise of the children leaving the elementary school in front of my office becomes deafening. I think they are like birds liberated from their cages.

Giorgio speaks easily, saying that his parents are separating and that his father has already moved away from their flat. He doesn't like it, but it's ok. In those few seconds of silence, I notice that he doesn't look at his parents but only at me. I can see that he is a bit worried. After he speaks, there are another few moments of silence. Giorgio then asks if I could speak to his parents without him because they have their issues (it is exactly what he says) and maybe it's better that I listen to them without him. I'm surprised but I accept this, so I accompany him to the other room in my office, where he will not be able to hear us. When I return, the father is looking down at his hands, and I realize he has been doing this since the beginning of the session. The mother looks at me with anxious expectation.

The story of the parental couple: the father, P, is more than 25 years older than the mother. She came to Italy to work as a waitress in a night club and fell in love with P, a regular customer of the club. They had the child quite soon and went to live together. P has a family with grownup children. The eldest son, working in the same lucrative business agency owned by his parents, has a son only two years younger than Giorgio. Signor P, contrary to what he had promised to A, the mother of Giorgio, never divorced his previous wife. This situation has become unbearable for her. She adds that she doesn't complain about the financial arrangements for Giorgio or for herself, but she feels she has been cheated and wants to be repaid (not clear in which sense). When I ask about their son, the father says that he loves this child who has arrived so late in life. It makes him proud to see him so beautiful and so loving towards him, and he wishes to do whatever is possible to preserve the integrity of the son. He also admits that maybe it was selfish to have a child at his age and with such a young woman, but it was irresistible for him: "It was like returning to my thirties." A. seems moved, but dry-eyed and undeterred. She says that her life had been ruined. Luckily Giorgio gives her a reason for living.

We are near the end of the session, and I suggest that they find a sympathetic lawyer to settle their separation issues, that what is important is that they love their child and that I will see them again after I have had two or three sessions with Giorgio. If they wish, I will give them the phone numbers of some colleagues who could help to solve their own problems and to develop their parenting skills.

When we finish talking, they thank me. I felt that they really meant it and asked myself why? Gratitude? Maybe the reason was that I really felt sympathetic with them and didn't judge their situation. They were two people with their own issues, with unclear intentions towards their son, but had space in themselves for some understanding. For the moment, that was enough. Giorgio returned to my room and he seemed relieved. We agreed to have another session in a few days. They left.

My office had returned to silence, the school children with their loud singing had filled the square by now and had disappeared with their retinue of babysitters, mothers and grandparents. Giorgio's sensory impression reappeared in a lonely light, and I recognized a dark sadness in his beautiful dark eyes and face.

Following our initial meeting, the parents went to separate parent support groups, which was their choice. The mother at a certain point also started her own therapy.

Giorgio worked with me for about two years. We rarely spoke directly of his parents. We engaged in his life, gave space to drawing, playing, inventing stories, and using fairy tales that threaded through our encounters. When I asked about his preferred fairytale, he answered he didn't have one, that he knew about them but had discovered them only when he went to school. Giorgio had not gone to kindergarten.

It was soon clear that the love the mother declared was mixed with her need for security. I could empathize with her but not at the expense of the child. The falling in love of any mother with her marvelous son favors at the beginning the embryonic development of the *subjective sense of self*. Fundamental in the process of becoming the subject is the perception of the separateness of the other. This differentiation is the road towards subjectivity and individuation. Gradually from the initial symbiotic relationship, mother and child discover their separateness. In the process, the position of the mother or the caregiver is of central importance.

From the declaration of the mother in the first visit, Giorgio gave the impression or a sort of reverie of a child that had to emancipate from the close and in some ways suffocating relationship with the mother. Giorgio represented for his mother the security of a better future. His father had legally recognized him, so he had the same rights as the son and daughter born in his father's marriage. Economic security was granted by his birth and this was a reassurance for the mother. I felt sympathetic with her. If you are discriminated against and fear being expelled by the country where you have found a better life, you are anxious to keep that security for you and your child. The father's reassurances were not enough and who could blame her--she needed time to adjust to the new situation which was so different from what she was expecting.

The problem that emerged from the first session in the countertransference was Giorgio's perfection, the *divine child* who had to repair the world of the parents. The child met the expectations of his parents. He saved his mother and rejuvenated his father. Even I, as his analyst, was dazzled by the *divine child* archetype and in the heat of the first encounter had missed the darkness of depression that was the reason for the visit.

Giorgio's mother saw in her son the possibility of making a dream come true. Every good-enough mother can see in her child the *marvelous baby*. In their presence I was captured by the promise he represented. As the perfect child, he had the function of saving his parents, the father from old age, the mother from the lack of status and the discrimination that goes with it, especially if you are a young woman working in a night club whose only bargaining chips are youth and beauty.

The mother, by idealizing her love for him, kept him imprisoned in her projections. The father was not very helpful in creating the triangulation that could help the separation from the mother. Stern[7] suggested that maternal love and *attunement* foster the subjective sense of self. Attunement is the first and fundamental step in the process of becoming a subject. Attunement should foster and support otherness and differentiation. The mother in the primary relationship should gradually separate from her child by recognizing her own efforts and frustrations as well as the shadow aspects of her maternal love. Thus, she establishes limits for herself but also for the child who, through the small frustrations necessary to delimit his boundaries, will recognize the difference between inside and outside, will experience separateness and develop thoughts about oneself and the world.

---

[7] D. Stern, *The Interpersonal World of the Infant.*

Brigitte Allain Dupré makes a distinction between devotion (dévotion) and dedication (dévouement). Devotion has a religious connotation. It therefore has the component of the adoration of the child as the savior. Dedication is the attention given to the child, the recognition of his or her needs as different from that of the mother or the caregiver. She will not be saved by the child but will grow with him or her and will help the child's differentiation.

Being aware that around Giorgio the archetype of the *divine child* could easily constellate, made it possible for me to differentiate his real needs from those of the adults around him. The negative and evil, including aggression, had an important part in the analytic process. I helped Giorgio explore the intricacy of his feelings towards his parents but also towards his half-brothers and sister who, like ghosts, hung over his psyche, creating nightmares and fears of being devoured.

## Conclusions

After choosing to discuss Giorgio I wondered if my choice had been dictated by my association to my little friend on the beach. At the onset of puberty, children start to change physically, mentally and psychologically. The issues that haven't been resolved or went wrong in infancy will return amplified, in search of solution. For this reason, it is extremely important to give attention to children of Giorgio's age.

According to the World Health Organization, the years of puberty and early adolescence are particularly important in the prevention of severe psychiatric diseases which start to manifest at prepubertal and pubertal ages. In Italy, pediatricians have an important role. Pediatric care is free to the age of 18, including psychological and psychiatric consultations. Pediatricians can identify situations of discomfort, guiding and referring parents for treatment.

In Milan I collaborate with a center that offers to prepubertal children, adolescents and their parents support in this special period of life. The center is supported by the Red Cross, private donors, and the University of Milan. Its primary aim is to prevent the onset of more serious pathologies later in life. The colleagues of the center work to sensitize pediatricians to the prodromes of psychological uneasiness. At the time of my work with Giorgio the center did not exist. I was lucky that his parents agreed to work on themselves.

I would like to conclude this chapter first by emphasizing that the international network of child psychology is vital to Analytical Psychology and psychoanalysis. In Italy, the first steps in what would become child and adolescent Analytical Psychology were made with special attention to the world beyond the Alps.

Second, work with children has a lot to teach Analytical Psychology in general. The knowledge accumulated by psychoanalysis and Analytical Psychology in the field is important not only because childhood suffering lives on in the adult patient, or because the archaic-archetypal contents are first met and activated in childhood. There is much more that our Jungian work with children elucidates.

In this therapeutic work we play, we create "*as if*" worlds and stories which help to explore the resources that lie unexplored in the recesses of trauma. Entering with the lightness offered by pre-symbolic thought into these closed-off areas allows us to explore the messy uneasiness of the archaic layers which reverberate and disturb development. With an approach that is light in using interpretation, we may discover potentially creative resources.

Finally, as Albert Ciccone ably states, analyzing the contribution of what child analysis brings to psychoanalytic work with adults suggests that exploring through playing and creativity allows the emergence of aspects of the Self. From a Jungian perspective, child analysis grounds us in helping the process of differentiation on the road to individuation.

## REFERENCES

Bernhard E. *Mitobiografia* [*Mythobiography*]. Biblioteca Adelphi, 1969.
Bisagni, F. *Io non sono nulla. Riflessioni psicoanalitiche su bambini e uomini d'oggi. [I am not Nothing. Psychoanalytic Reflections on Children and Adults of Today].* Milan, Italy: Vivarium., 2006.

Bisagni, F., Fina, N. &Vezzoli, C. (Eds.). *Jung Today. Vol. 2: Childhood and Adolescence.* Hauppauge, NY: Nova Science Publisher, 2009.

—— On the Impact of Words. Interpretation, Empathy and Affect Regulation. *Journal of Analytical. Psychology, 58,* 5, 615-635, 2012.

Bosio W. Mariella Gambino Loriga (1920-2006), Pioniera della psicologia Analitica Infantile l'asilo di Villetta Casana. In *Enkelados, 6:* 2017, Nuova Ipsoa Editore.

Cambray, J. Un cas pour la rencontre entre analystes freudiens et anaystes jungiens sur les archétypes et/ou fantasme originaires. *Le Cahiers Jungiens de Psychanalyse, 1,* 133, 10-19, 2011.

Ciccone, A. *La psicoanalisi a prova di bambino [Child-Proof Psychoanalysis].* Alpes Italia srl., 2019.

Di Montezemolo, A. Ernst Bernhard e Due Maestri del Cinema Italiano: Vittorio De Seta e Federico Fellini. In *Enkelados, 6:* 2017, Nuova Ipsoa Editore.

Eco, U. *Il Fascismo Eterno [the Eternal Fascism].* La nave di Teseo, 2018.

Fordham, M. Notes for the Formation of a Model of Infant Development. *Journal of Analytical Psychology, 38,* 1, 5-12, 1993.

Jung, C.G. *Children's Dreams. Notes on the Seminars given in 1936-1940.* Princeton, NJ: Princeton University Press, 2012.

Madera, R. (Ed.). Maestri Scomodi, *Rivista di Psicologia Analitica, 2,* 1966.

Montecchi, F. (Ed.). *I simboli dell'infanzia. Dal pensiero di Jung al lavoro clinico coi bambini.* Rome, Italy: La Nuova Italia Scientifica, 1995.

Nagliero, G. & Grosso, W. (Eds.). *Analisi in età evolutiva.* Milan, Italy: Vivarium, 2008.

Neumann, E. *The Child: Structure and Dynamics of the Nascent Personality.* London, UK: Hodder and Stoughton, 1973.

Sidoli, M., Davis, M. *Jungian Child Psychotherapy.* London, UK: Karnac Books, 1988.

Sidoli M. & Bovensiepen, G. Incest Fantasies and Self-Destructive Acts. *Jungian and Post-Jungian Psychotherapy in Adolescence.* London, UK: Routledge, Taylor & Francis Group, 1995.

Solomon, H. *The Self in Transformation.* London, UK: Routledge, 2007.

Stern, D. *The Interpersonal World of the Infant.* London, UK: Karnac Books, 1998.

Tustin, F. *Autistic States in Children.* London, UK: Routledge and Kegan Paul, 1981.

Turinese L. La Psicologia Oracolare di Bianca Garufi. In *Enkelados, 6,* Nuova Ipsoa Editore, 2017.

Von Franz, M. *Interpretation of Fairy Tales.* Boston, MA & London, UK: Shambala Books, 1996.

# CHAPTER 3

## This Land Was Made for You and Me:[1]
## Encountering the Other in the
## United States of America
### *Audrey Punnett*
#### Fresno, California

> We hold these truths to be self-evident, that all men are
> created equal, that they are endowed by their Creator with
> certain unalienable Rights, that among these are Life,
> Liberty and the pursuit of Happiness.[2]

THIS QUOTATION, FROM THE Declaration on Independence,
signed July 4, 1776, pronounced the thirteen American colonies at war
with Great Britain as thirteen independent sovereign states no longer
under British rule. These states had taken the first step toward forming
the United States of America. While this is a foundational statement
about human rights in the United States, it does not reflect the earlier
history and shadow of this country.

Another foundational element, the Statue of Liberty, was dedicated
in 1886 as an icon for freedom and the belief that democracy prevailed
in the United States. The Statue of Liberty, a gift from France, sits on
Liberty Island, a strategic location because vessels arriving in New York
had to sail past it to dock at nearby Ellis Island, a major port of entry from

---

[1] W. Guthrie. *This Land is Your Land.*
[2] National Archives, America's Founding Documents, Declaration of Independence
Transcript.

1892 — 1924 for millions of European immigrants. Emma Lazarus's poem, *The New Colossus*, with its famous lines, "Give me your tired, your poor, your huddled masses yearning to breathe free,"[3] was inscribed on a bronze plaque at the Statue in 1903. The statue and Lazarus's words welcomed immigrants, yet throughout American history, many immigrants were seen as "the Other," despite words and statues to the contrary.

## THE CULTURE

### Background

The first permanent English settlement in North America was Jamestown, in Virginia in 1607, followed by Plymouth, in Massachusetts in 1620. Several factors led to these settlements. Earlier Spanish colonization showed the English what treasures could be extracted from the New World. England was burdened by a burgeoning, increasingly poor and landless population. English colonization was also influenced by the Protestant Reformation: dissident Protestants and persecuted Catholics were looking for a more desirable place to live. A charter from King James I of England established Jamestown, which, after trying times, became a permanent settlement with the help of the local Native Americans. It was only a few years later, in 1619, when a Dutch warship appeared off Jamestown and sold some twenty Africans to the English. This sale marks a beginning of disregard for other human beings and of the shadow that continues to exist in the United States.

Dehumanization of Africans brought to the U.S. to be enslaved, their enslaved descendants, and free African-Americans was progressive, with increasingly restrictive and punitive laws ruling those of African descent, continuing until 1863. Brutal working conditions, harsh or lethal punishments, separation of families, and forced sexual relations between enslavers and enslaved people characterized conditions for those with even "one drop" of African ancestry. Attempts to escape or rebel were met by torture or death.

---

[3] B. Parent. What is the Quote on the Statue of Liberty?

The founding fathers built America on slavery. It was legal in each of the thirteen colonies. In fact, the White House where the President lives was built by enslaved African-Americans. Despite being legally defined as property from 1619 — 1862, enslaved African-Americans understood that the freedom and equality promised by the Declaration of Independence was their right.

The outbreak of Civil War (1861-1865) plunged the Unites States into chaos. On September 22, 1862, President Abraham Lincoln issued the Emancipation Proclamation to end slavery. However, it was not until the 13th, 14th and 15th Amendments to the Constitution were passed by Congress between 1865 and 1870, that African-Americans were granted full rights as citizens of the United States.

The era of Reconstruction, in which African-Americans voted, held public office, and enjoyed other rights granted to European-Americans, lasted only from 1865 until early 1877. From then, until the passage of the Civil Rights legislation of the 1960's, African-Americans, especially in the Southern states which had seceded from the Union during the Civil War, faced ever-increasing restrictions on owning property, voting, obtaining education, using public transportation, and other rights. In 1896, the landmark Supreme Court decision of Plessy vs. Ferguson established the doctrine of "separate but equal," which codified these restrictive laws, which became known as "Jim Crow."

In the Southern states, and to some extent in the Northern states, "separate but equal" segregation became brutal. The Jim Crow system of laws and code of conduct kept African- Americans as second-class citizens. Lynchings became one method for enforcing Jim Crow, terrorizing the African-American community and reinforcing the notion of white supremacy. As a result, over six million African-Americans in the Southern states, from 1916 until 1970, moved away from the South to the Northeast, Midwest and West. This movement became known as "The Great Migration."

W.E.B. Du Bois, 1868 – 1963, a famous African-American intellectual, helped create a counter-narrative to negate African-American stereotypes. With other noted African-Americans, he established the Niagara

Movement in 1905, which became a basis for the modern civil rights movement, and also co-founded the Association for the Advancement of Colored People (NAACP) in 1909, which remains a leading civil rights organization.[4]

After World War I, African-Americans began to become better known on the cultural front to European-Americans through literature, music— jazz and blues—and art. Harlem, in New York City, became a mecca of African-American culture, and many African-American artists migrated there. At the same time, however, the Ku Klux Klan (KKK) revived in the South to defend white supremacy. Around the nation, African-American communities were targeted, people murdered, businesses and residences and whole communities torched, as European-Americans strove to maintain hegemony over good jobs, good housing and good education.

The American Armed Forces were not integrated until 1948, and segregated schools were outlawed only in 1954, with the Supreme Court decision, Brown vs. Board of Education, although this law was not fully implemented in the South until the late 1960's. Today, however, although segregation is illegal in public schools, "white flight," the desertion of European-American families to private schools and to expensive suburbs, means that over 60 percent of African-American students remain in de-facto segregated schools.[5]

Although African-Americans strove continuously for rights accorded European-Americans and saw gains in some areas, a marker for the American Civil Rights movement came in December 1955, when Rosa Parks refused to give up her seat on a city bus to a white man in Montgomery, Alabama and move to the section specified for African-Americans. Her action led to a boycott by African-Americans of public transport in Montgomery, which ultimately led to desegregation of the transport system. This boycott launched a revolution, and her challenge to segregation become a people's movement, led by Dr. Martin Luther King, Jr.

---

[4] J. Anderson, H. L. Gates, P. Kunhardt & D. McGee. The African Americans: Many Rivers to Cross with Henry Louis Gates, Jr.

[5] E. Garcia, Schools are Still Segregated, and Black Children are Paying the Price.

Following the principles of nonviolence of India's Mahatma Gandhi and of nonviolent leaders in the United States, Dr. King advocated civil disobedience as the most powerful way to effect change. From 1955 until 1964, when President Lyndon Johnson signed the Civil Rights Act and 1965, when he signed the Voting Rights Act, Dr. King and others organized marches, boycotts, and other nonviolent protests against segregation of African-Americans. However, when Dr. King was assassinated in 1968, many African-Americans lost faith that racial equality could be achieved through non-violence.

While the Watts uprising against police maltreatment in Los Angeles in 1965 had presaged the uprising by African-Americans in cities around the country following Dr. King's assassination, these uprisings exemplified the hopelessness and anger of many in the African-American community about the systematic denial of equal rights they had felt throughout their lifetimes.

Unfortunately, although increasing numbers of African-Americans have completed higher education, and segregation in housing is forbidden by law, everywhere African-Americans turn, they see discrimination—in racial profiling by the police, in incarceration disproportionate to their numbers in the population, to ceilings in job opportunities, in de facto housing segregation, in recent attempts to restrict voting rights, etc. Peaceful demonstrations as well as uprisings with loss of property and life continue in response to these injustices. Having an African-American President in the While House from 2008 – 2016 has not stopped the daily indignities experienced by African-Americans. The journey from slave ship to White House, from bondage to full equality continues to be long and perilous.

While I have highlighted brutality, exploitation and discrimination towards African-Americans, Native Americans, who settled North America millennia before European-Americans arrived, experienced this same denial of human rights. Originally hunters and gatherers from Asia, they started farming in North America by 7000 BCE and lived in highly ordered and complex societies.

Starting in 1513, Spain, France, England, and Russia colonized North

America for many reasons, from territorial acquisition to extracting saleable goods as well as forcing Native American "heathens" to abandon their spiritual beliefs and adopt Christianity. In the nineteenth century, the United States government disenfranchised practically all North American tribes of their land and sovereignty.[6] Native Americans were forcibly relocated to less desirable lands, confined to reservations or slaughtered. By U.S. law, Native American children were to be assimilated into "white," European-American culture by sending them away from their families to distant residential schools, where they experienced maltreatment, were harshly punished for speaking their language, and often became ill and died, due to crowded conditions and poor medical care. Many of these federal policies were not fully discontinued until the Civil Rights movement of the 1960's and 1970's. Native Americans are now demanding their rights as a historically oppressed minority victimized by imperial conquest[7].

Asian-Americans have experienced discrimination throughout United States history, starting with restrictions on becoming citizens in 1790, restrictions on immigration and land ownership in the nineteenth and twentieth centuries and culminating in the removal of American citizens of Japanese descent to internment camps during World War II following the bombing of Pearl Harbor in 1941. They were forced by the government to abandon their homes and work and move under military armed guard to remote heavily guarded detention camps within the Western United States.

Racism in California against Chinese workers, who came during the Gold Rush in the 1850's and helped build the Transcontinental Railroad, completed in 1869, culminated in the Chinese Exclusion Law passed in 1882 by the U.S Congress.[8] This law persisted into the 1940's.

There are numerous other minorities in the United States who have experienced and continue to experience discrimination, the details of which are beyond the scope of this chapter.

---

[6] E. P. Pauls, American Indian, *Encyclopedia Britannica*.

[7] F. Flavin, *Native Americans and American History*.

[8] J. Burton, M. Farrell, F. Lord & R. Lord. A brief history of Japanese American Relocation during World War II.

In addition, we have the Judeo-Christian God-image that is related to the Puritan cultural complex which embodies strict judgment of others' sexual and ethical morality and the absence of any awareness of one's power shadow[9] on which this country was founded.

## The Other

The United States as an ethnically diverse culture has impacted both positively and negatively on the cultural racial complexes that have developed in the unconscious by way of archetypal energies.[10] As such, complexes can begin at an early age from child-rearing practices and later through individual experiences. The parenting of children thus plays an important role in attitudes and values toward the Other, i.e., the one who is different from us.

Jung states,

> The vast majority of people are quite incapable of putting themselves individually into the minds of another.... Even the man who we think we know best and who assures us himself that we understand him through and through is at bottom a stranger to us. He is *different*. The most we can do, and the best, is to have at least some inkling of his otherness, to respect it....[11]

A recent article by Karen Naifeh illustrates the prevalence of the white shadow in America. She makes the case that culture shapes consciousness and that this nation created a story that racial differences existed, and the white race was superior to all others. This story kept "in the shadows the political and economic rationale for oppression in a country whose founding principle was equality of all men."[12] What has gone unrecognized is one of Jung's basic tenets that the most envied or bitterest foe

---

[9] M. Roy. When a Religious Archetype Becomes a Cultural Complex: Puritanism in America. *The Cultural Complex.*

[10] F. Brewster. *The Racial Complex: A Jungian perspective on culture and race.*

[11] C.G. Jung, The Relations Between the Ego and the Unconscious, *Two Essays on Analytical Psychology, CW 7*, ¶ 363.

[12] K. Naifeh. Encountering the Other: The White Shadow, *Jung Journal: Culture & Psyche*, 13.

is not that one worst enemy but the "other self" that dwells within the person.[13]. We see this continually in the projecting of our own shadow onto the Other who is different or alien to us. The healing must include the withdrawing of the projection from the Other and in the case of the child, strengthening the child's ego to withstand negative assaults or aggression from others as well as to overcome internalized feelings of being "less than" or "other."

Strengthening the ego involves accepting ourselves as we are, involving those aspects of self-esteem which include: a sense of security, a sense of identity, a sense of belonging, a sense of purpose and a sense of personal competence. As we shall see in the case discussed later in the chapter, strengthening these aspects of self-esteem was key to healing for this child. Also, over time and as the child matures, developing empathy for the Other is critical.

## Jungian Child Analysis in America

The founding of the first analytical psychological training in the United States began in 1943 with the founding of the Medical Society for Analytical Psychology in San Francisco, California. In 1950 it merged with the Association of Clinical Analytical Psychologists and became the Society of Jungian Analysts of Northern California. On July 13, 1964, the Society established the C.G. Jung Institute of San Francisco as a nonprofit organization listing as its primary function the operation of a low fee clinic and its secondary function education and the training of analysts. Training of analysts became primary and the operation of a low fee clinic became secondary, following an amendment to the articles of incorporation on March 16, 1977.[14] The second C.G. Jung Institute to be founded was in Zurich on April 24, 1948.

In the beginning, the primary emphasis was on adult training and the training for child analysts lagged, in part due to the focus by Jung on the adult. Nevertheless, one finds clinical observations and ideas regarding

---

[13] C.G. Jung, *CW 7.*
[14] Richard Willets, personal communication, September 13, 2021.

the self and the mother-infant relationship[15] in Jung's writings. Initially, Jung discussed reconstructed memories and dreams from childhood as recalled by adults whom Jung analyzed. Later, Jungians began the direct observation and study of the inner workings of the child which continues today.

Frances Wickes, Eric Neumann and Michael Fordham were leaders in writing about the work with children. Through a generous gift from Frances Wickes to the San Francisco Institute the interest in child training began. In the late 1970's one of the candidates, who was a child psychiatrist, undertook the London training with Michael Fordham. Following this there was a movement towards the development of a program in San Francisco. Many child-oriented conferences and seminars were held over the years, as well as multiple visits and consultations by Fordham and others.

In 2000 a child study group/colloquium was formed in San Francisco to discuss work with children. Then in 2007 an Ad Hoc infant, child, adolescent training (iCAT) committee was created with the approval of the International Association for Analytical Psychology (IAAP); iCAT became a formal training program in 2010. The training is a two-year program consisting of one year of infant observation and one year of didactics with ongoing consultation of cases with both children and adolescents, as well as two required Control Case papers, one on a child and one on an adolescent. The child training integrates with the adult training, for those who have applied and been accepted into the child training. Currently the San Francisco Institute has fourteen child analysts who were grandfathered in as child analysts and one who was formally trained as a child analyst in Zurich.

Similarly in Los Angeles, a group was being formed in the 1940's, forming the Analytical Psychology Club which served as a source of lectures about Jung's work at that time. On January 10, 1953 a letter from Jung recognized the Club as a center for research and training in

---

[15] M. Leahy, Jung and the Post-Jungians on the Theory of Jungian Child Analysis, *Jungian Child Analysis.*

analytical psychology. In December 1978, the Hilde Kirsch Children's Center was founded.[16] It was established to support those working with children and primarily how the development of the psyche can be applied to the therapeutic treatment of children and adolescents. The Center provides low-cost Jungian therapy to children in the Los Angeles area.

From 2005-2006, the C.G. Jung Institute of Los Angeles also grand-fathered in those analysts who had been working with children. A formal training program began in October, 2005.[17] Including those certified by the Institute, there are currently seventeen certified Jungian child analyst members of the Los Angeles Institute. The training program is open to those who have become certified as an adult analyst. Currently the program is custom-tailored to each child analyst in training, with a Control Case paper written as part of the requirement for certification. There are no other known formal child analytic training programs in the United States.

## The Family

The "American" family (i.e., the family whose ancestors came from the Protestant countries of Northern and Western Europe, and France, hence "White") experienced changes in structure and function from the period of colonization through later westward expansion, indus-trialization, urbanization, and modernization.[18] During the colonial period, this European-American family unit provided the setting for economic, educational, social, recreational, and religious functions. It was patriarchal, and extended family would live nearby. Male children grew up with the expectation they would acquire the family land or business, if there was one.

Puritanism was prevalent with emphasis on hard work, prudence, avoidance of ritual and display, rigorous caste lines and repression of

---

[16] Hilde Kirsch Children's Center, Jung Institute Los Angeles, https://junginla.org/clinical-services/hilde-kirsch-childrens-center/

[17] Gloria Avrech, personal communication, January 11, 2021.

[18] R. Habenstein & R.A. Olson. Families and Children in History, *Handbook of Clinical Child Psychology*.

emotions.[19] Families were large, and children contributed to the work; they were expected to obey their parents and often were harshly punished.

With the advent of the Industrial Revolution in the nineteenth century, changes began to occur in the European-American family structure. Immigrants from Europe began working in textile mills, mines and factories, as well as in agriculture. For the non-agricultural sector, the home became increasingly separate from the workplace. Children as young as seven or eight years old began working in often dangerous workplace environments. Thus, industrialization lessened the protective functions of the family. Parents and their children hoped to better their place in society through education and accumulating wealth. Towards the end of the nineteenth century, more women were entering the workforce and gaining the right to own property. Parental involvement in the teaching of children was diminished due to public education now available. The concept of adolescence emerged during this period as a stage in child development.

In 1914, the U.S. Children's Bureau published the first edition of *Infant Care* to assist parents with childrearing.[20] Other editions followed, with suggestions now leaving the philosophy and ideals of parenting to the parents' own preconceptions in general leaning toward leniency and understanding of the child's behavior.

In the early twentieth century, only twenty percent of European-American women worked outside the home. Those who did were primarily young and unmarried. The percentage of African-American women working outside the home was at least double that of European-American women. Although most women had limited occupational opportunities, their numbers helped support the so-called first wave of the women's movement, dating back to 1848, when primarily European-American women came together to advocate for change on a variety of social issues, including suffrage and temperance, culminating in the ratification of

---

[19] R. Habenstein & R.A. Olson. Families and Children in History, *Handbook of Clinical Child Psychology.*

[20] R. Habenstein & R.A. Olson. Families and Children in History, *Handbook of Clinical Child Psychology.*

the Nineteenth Amendment to the Constitution in 1920, guaranteeing women the right to vote.

When the Japanese attacked Pearl Harbor on December 7, 1941, the lives of many Americans changed, when men were mobilized into the military, leaving their peacetime jobs.[21] A recruitment campaign was initiated with a fictional character, "Rosie the Riveter," used to encourage women into the job market. "Rosie" embodied courage and wisdom, strength and conviction, and the desire to make the world a better place. The campaign was successful. It emphasized hardworking women discovering new talents and developing greater confidence in their capabilities. Merging with longer term trends by 1970, 50 percent of single women and 40 percent of married women were participating in the labor force. By 2020, 75 percent of working-age women (ages 25-54) were in the labor force, as opposed to 88 percent of working-age men. While women are becoming more highly educated and are entering fields formerly dominated by men, they still earn about 10-17% less than men on the average.

In the U.S., women are less likely than men to reach the highest echelons in the corporate world and the professions. In addition to overt discrimination against women, primary limiting factors include that such fields require longer working hours, and one is penalized for taking time off for child-bearing or other child-related responsibilities. These factors primarily affect women, who continue to bear the most responsibility for domestic roles and child-rearing. Some changes are happening with job sharing, cross training and flexible scheduling, but these changes can also create difficulties in scheduling childcare, which is affordable for fewer than half of all families.[22]

---

[21] Bright Hub Education, How World War II Led Women to Enter the Workforce, November 5, 2010. https://www.brighthubeducation.com/history-homework-help/94437-world-war-ii-women-in-the-workforce/

[22] J.L. Yellen, The History of Women's Work and Wages and How it has Creates Success for Us All, May 2020. https://www.brookings.edu/essay/the-history-of-womens-work-and-wages-and-how-it-has-created-success-for-us-all/

## Child Care

The United States is the only industrialized nation among 42 countries analyzed by the Organization for Economic Cooperation and Development (OECD) that does not have any mandated paid parental leave policy.[23] The Family Medical and Leave Act of 1993 (FMLA) provides up to twelve weeks of unpaid job-protected leave for workers to care for a family member with serious health conditions or for children who were just born or adopted. However only about 60% of the workforce is eligible[24] The Federal Employee Paid Leave Act took effect in October of 2020. It grants federal employees twelve weeks of paid parental leave for the birth or foster or adoptive placement of a child. Currently, nine states have enacted some form of paid family and medical leave.[25]

Nearly one in four children in the United States are being raised by single mothers, yet childcare is unaffordable for many, and as outlined above, paid leave for most parents is not available. In fact, working parents with children in childcare pay nearly twice as much of their income (23.1%) verses the OECD average (11.8%).[26]

While childcare and education are heavily underwritten by the government in other wealthy countries, in the United States only about half of all children between the ages of three to six are getting publicly supported childcare. Nevertheless, the US ranks higher in the percentage of infants and toddlers in formal childcare, partly because we do not offer paid maternity leave for mothers and few extended families are available to help.

---

[23] S.N. Johnson, Stracker News, March 2, 2021, Here's How Much Parental Leave You Get in Every U.S. State. *Newsweek.* https://www.newsweek.com/heres-how-much-parental-leave-you-get-every-us-state-1573213

[24] Women's Health Policy. Paid Family and Sick Leave in the U.S., December 14, 2020. https://www.kff.org/womens-health-policy/fact-sheet/paid-family-leave-and-sick-days-in-the-u-s/

[25] Women's Health Policy Paid Family and Sick Leave in the U.S. December 14, 2020. https://www.kff.org/womens-health-policy/fact-sheet/paid-family-leave-and-sick-days-in-the-u-s/

[26] S. Mead, Child Care Laggard, *U.S. News and World Report*, February 23, 2017. https://www.usnews.com/opinion/knowledge-bank/articles/2017-02-23/the-us-is-a-laggard-on-child-care

A review of childcare by Plumer in 2013,[27] revealed that most American day care centers are rated "fair" or "poor" due to their child-to-provider ratio. Although childcare remains extremely expensive for many families, childcare workers are often paid poorly and are minimally trained. State regulators do not have enough people to inspect facilities regularly and often face pressure to keep centers open regardless of conditions.

De Mause[28] outlines Western European cultural attitudes that have prevailed in the raising of children from the Middle Ages to the late twentieth century. In the twentieth century, cultural attitudes have moved towards more empathy and more feeling for the child. Ideally, parents are involved in empathizing with the child and emphasizing that the child knows what they need in each stage of life. In my practice I have found, however, I often need to help parents set age-appropriate boundaries, as children and adolescents are frequently given far too much latitude, which allows for little enjoyment for their current chronological age.

In addition, we are in an age where cultural diversity has been named and increasingly valued. As an analyst, I must be ever attentive to validate and affirm the cultural diversity of my clients and of my community, to be aware of how the American shadow of the "Other" impacts everyone I see and how keeping that shadow in mind informs my work.

## The Therapy

In this section, I will discuss working with a child and family who had been "othered" in two ways: as dark-skinned, in a society whose dominant culture devalues and discriminates against those with skin darker than "White" European-Americans, and as immigrants, non-English-speaking in the home, and bearing different cultural values about family structure and obligation from the dominant culture around them.

In my work with children, I meet with the parents first to gain knowledge about the problem, but also to learn about the family structure and

---

[27] B. Plumer, Five Shocking Facts About Child Care in the United States, *The Washington Post,* April 15, 2013. https://www.washingtonpost.com/news/wonk/wp/2013/04/15/five-shocking-facts-about-child-care-in-the-united-states/

[28] L. De Maus, *The History of Childhood.*

the flexibility within that structure. This initial meeting is important because parents need to understand and integrate within themselves the changes within the child as the therapy progresses, and I begin to learn, starting from this first meeting, how best to help them do that. After the initial meeting with the parents, I then meet with the child for several sessions and then lastly, I meet again with the parents to formulate the problem and what is needed. This sequence has served as a good working model which places the parents as team members in the treatment of their child. My recommendations at that time may include various options, including seeing the child individually, working with the parents and/ or working with the family.

## Anand

Anand (pseudonym) a nearly five-year-old boy of South Asian background was referred by his pediatrician. His mother first contacted me when he was three, stating she thought she may have an issue because she was trying to increase his self-esteem and he remained clingy to her. She later cancelled that appointment because her husband could not attend and said she would call back. Nearly two years later she called again to make an appointment.

My work with families of South Asian background had been rewarding in the past and for the most part centered on improving parenting skills. My paternal grandfather was born in this family's country of origin, and I had always enjoyed working with families coming from there because I felt a link to them through my grandfather. This case was different due to its length and to my more intense involvement with the family. In my work with them, I needed to be aware at every moment of the cultural boundaries within the family structure, supporting the mother and father in their respective roles, as well as Anand's emotional growth. In addition, I became more aware of how my family background might influence my work with them. When my grandfather lived there, the British ruled, to the general population's detriment. I wondered how my feelings about that history might play out in my work with this family. I wondered if they would view me as "the Other." Anand's parents were clearly trying to assimilate into "American" culture and I wondered how they would view me, in their struggles to assimilate.

At my first meeting with the parents, they described Anand as "mischievous, hyperactive, and not controlling his body movements." At his private, academically-oriented, predominantly "white" pre-kindergarten, he hit other children. He had only recently begun using words at school to express his feelings; English was his second language. He seemed oppositional to learning his ABC's and would easily become frustrated. He would have daytime accidents at school and would say, "I'm a bad kid." He complained the other children "don't like me." As I listened to his parents, I heard them describe a child who did not fit in with the children nor meet the expectations of the teachers. I wondered how their "Otherness" affected them and Anand as they struggled with his school problems. The parents had become frustrated but also did not know how to help their son.

Anand's mother and father had moved to the United States with their parents, when they were very young. Their marriage was a traditional arranged marriage, which they both described as satisfactory and said they loved one another. They lived with the father's family, including for Anand, a paternal great-grandfather, two paternal grandparents, a paternal uncle, his parents, his older sister, and at the time of the referral, a younger sibling about to be born.

Anand's father was the eldest of three brothers and was expected to assume the family business in which he worked. He was devoted to doing as his father wished and to take on more and more responsibility for the business, which involved investing his time and energy. Anand's mother was employed full-time outside the family business and contributed financially to the household, which was helpful since the father received no salary. Anand's father was compensated by the family living rent-free in Anand's grandparents' home and by having other benefits, such as childcare and having meals prepared by the extended family. Anand's parents, except for two years, had always lived in this multigenerational setting. His mother expressed more frustration with this arrangement than his father. Anand's mother had one elder brother who was married with children and who lived with Anand's maternal grandparents.

Anand's mother's family came from wealth in their country of origin but lost this due to her grandfather's poor decision-making, which cost them all their land holdings. They initially worked in low-paying jobs after coming to this country. Anand's mother was discriminated against in her family because of the darkness of her skin; her family feared they would not be able to find a husband for her. Thus, her own family "Othered" her, because of her dark skin. Anand's mother worked very hard to have her son fit in and not experience an inferiority complex as she did. With a college degree in business, she had taken a lower-level job in a different field to have a schedule that matched the children's school schedule. This job required a significant commute each day. Because of her own insecurities, she did poorly on interviews. Although she had been applying for several years for jobs closer to home, she had been consistently rejected.

The parents were married ten years at the time of the consultation. They had two children, an eight-year-old daughter, and Anand, nearly age five. A third child, a daughter, was born six months later. With this third child, the mother experienced a post-partum depression. She wanted no more children. Against her husband's wishes, she had a tubal ligation some years later, stating she had no emotional energy to give to another child. Anand was the only male child on both sides of the family in over thirty years, and because of his family's culture, quite revered as a result.

Anand was born full term. There were no problems with the pregnancy or delivery. He was breast-fed for eight weeks, when his mother returned to work. He achieved his developmental milestones on time. At the time of Anand's birth, his parents were living independently. They returned to live with the father's family when Anand was eighteen months of age, when another family member, with whom they had conflict, moved out. Because of surgery for an undescended testicle when he was fifteen months old and for a hernia at age three, his parents viewed Anand as a vulnerable child. As a baby he was described as "mellow" and "curious." He had a short phase of head-banging and when told no, he would protest; these behaviors occurred when the family returned to the grandparents' home. At age three, when he entered preschool, he went through a biting stage.

Anand attended that preschool for one year and since the family did not primarily speak English in the home, he began learning English only when he began preschool. At age four, his parents moved Anand to a private pre-kindergarten, mentioned above. He had difficulty fitting in, not sitting still, constantly moving, and not following directions. He was not interested in learning his letters with his mother; she thought he would intentionally say his numbers incorrectly. He would have daytime accidents at school and would be teased by the children in the class for this. He wanted to be social with the other children but did not seem to know how to interact with them. His father tended to dismiss these issues saying, "He's a boy," but his mother was concerned, although it took her almost two years to insist that he been seen professionally.

When I first saw Anand, I initiated evaluations which Anand's mother pursued privately and through the public school system. These evaluations revealed he had delays in graphomotor skills, delayed gross and fine motor skills, and delayed sensory processing that affected his attention, coordination and balance. He was diagnosed with Attention Deficit Hyperactive Disorder and received medication for this with improved attention. With intervention, these areas all improved. Psychological testing when he entered the first grade in public school revealed verbal abilities in the superior range of intelligence and weakness in the visual-spatial-motor areas as previously diagnosed. He qualified for extra assistance with learning through the school and this assistance continued throughout the time he was seen.

These evaluations helped to aid my therapy. By knowing his strengths and weaknesses, I could help him understand and accept his limitations as well as help him learn compensating strategies. Anand's mother often became overinvolved with his homework and frustrated, lacking any patience to help him. I believed he also had a fair amount of anxiety which was exacerbated by his mother's frustration and criticalness.

When I first met with Anand, he willingly accompanied me to the playroom, separating easily from his father who brought him, since his mother was at work. He was a good-looking boy, although clearly not "White." For me, I welcomed his particular "Otherness." As mentioned above, because of my family connection to Anand's family's home country, I have always had a fondness for people from that country. Anand easily engaged in conversation but had some difficulty sitting still, with his body constantly in motion. He was also easily distracted. He complied with all that I requested of him, but would frequently make self-deprecatory remarks, e.g., "I don't know how to do that," and would give up, but with encouragement he would try, for example, to complete drawings.

When I gave him the House-Tree-Person Test, interestingly he described his house as a hotel in the forest, his tree as an apple tree, age six, with the apples falling off, and his person as himself "riding a shark bike feeling sad because I was driving to a hotel to see my Mom and Dad and whole family but I got lost in the forest." He shared a dream, which he stated was "bad:" "Somebody stole my treasures and broke them because he didn't like my treasures." When I asked him to draw his family, he included his great-grandfather, grandparents, parents and sister, omitting himself. In the drawing, his parents were preoccupied and the only one paying attention to him was his great-grandfather, who was going to surprise him with candy. He stated he did not like his current school because "other kids hit me there."

Since both parents worked, I learned the grandparents tended to the children in the mornings. They dressed Anand and often spoon-fed him. He had no responsibilities in the home. He slept with his great-grandfather. Although I realized that his grandparents dressing him and feeding him and his sleeping with his great-grandfather were probably normative within the family's culture, I found these facts disturbing. From my perspective, I saw infantilization of Anand and lack of appropriate boundary-setting between the generations. I wondered how I might intervene, within their culture, to provide an atmosphere for Anand which fostered his independence and agency.

I saw Anand for eight years, beginning with sessions every week and meeting with his parents frequently to address couple and family issues as well as assisting them with parenting. My decision to work with his parents in this way was due to the many professionals involved in Anand's care. It seemed prudent to keep the mental health care in one place and to help Anand's mother manage her anxiety in her efforts to seek out professionals to assist her son. As previously mentioned, I helped Anand's mother locate resources for the evaluations I believed Anand needed. I was becoming protective of her in wanting things to "go right," for Anand. I could sympathize with her struggle as a woman in a patriarchal society to find resources for her son. I understood her initial not calling back, when she did not receive support from her husband.

This brief background gives the picture of a complex family situation with multiple factors that needed attention outside of the presenting problems with Anand. Jung worked with the individual psyche that was moving toward wholeness in the second half of life. However, with Anand, I was working with cultural complexes and the psyches of Anand and his parents, and indirectly, other family members. It was crucial for me to maintain the involvement and cooperation of Anand's parents throughout the analysis of their child and to be aware, with every interaction I had with them, of the American cultural complex of the "Other."

In this case I saw the difficulties Anand's mother had suffered from rejection and discrimination for her skin color within her own family. Even when Anand was three, she was concerned with her son's self-esteem, but not until nearly two years later when the school noted her son's behavioral issues did she follow up on the referral. Only then, when the school—an authority external to the family—identified Anand's difficulties, did her husband support her decision to seek help. Without the school's disclosure of Anand's difficulties, Anand's mother had not been able to mobilize the family to seek help for Anand.

Anand's mother was keen on finding the latest and best interventions that would remediate her son's problems. Balancing her wish for his overcoming his problems with letting him be, and be who he was, was a challenge both for her and for me as I worked with her. However, as we worked together, she appreciated my honoring her feelings and what her investment in her son meant for him and for her. Later, she could mediate better among the many challenges she had set for herself around mothering and helping Anand so that he could better withstand the "Othering" she had faced in her own life.

Then there was Anand's father who was trying to please his parents and be the good son, but he was caught in this role and delegating parenting to the mother, which caused her anxiety. My understanding his frustration and offering ways he might better communicate with his wife was helpful. Anand's older sister did not have the pressure of being the male child in this family's culture. Like her mother, she was an excellent student and athlete.

With all this in mind, it was important for me to garner the parents' trust and to work with them as a team. Therefore, in the beginning I met with the parents to discuss some overall parenting strategies that would be helpful, specifically to increase individual time that each parent had with Anand, noticing his good behavior rather than focusing on the negative and to increase his self-help skills to promote his self-esteem. This was challenging for me as it involved gaining the cooperation of the paternal grandparents who were doing many things Anand could do on his own. I had to be able to enter the culture in a way that respected the elders and drew them into promoting Anand's self-esteem through acquiring new skills to prepare him for life. I channeled my frustrations towards the elders' infantilizing Anand and blurring boundaries by teaching the parents to model and teach others living in the family household, skills that could improve Anand's life.

The skills I was teaching were those I frequently use with families and thus this family no longer seemed "Other" to me, but rather a typical "American" family. For example, I suggested to his parents that Anand have some chores and awake independently with an alarm clock as he got older, suggestions I had made to many "American" families. We discussed ways they could approach the paternal grandparents with the new skills they were learning, for example, telling the grandparents that by giving Anand chores and responsibilities, they would be helping Anand to be more competent and self-assured. Anand's parents were successful in talking with the grandparents and implementing the changes.

While doing this work with his parents, I worked with Anand initially just to understand his stress. He seemed quite open to revealing his sufferings with the teasing he received at school and in his dream, with the loss of his personal "treasures" and feeling lost within the family. He later revealed what he experienced to be unprovoked harsh treatment by his father and mother, which seemed to be sparked by their frustration with his learning and physical difficulties.

He freely talked about the distress he experienced with other children who he perceived did not like him. Due to his physical, learning, and attentional difficulties he was socially awkward. He did not want to draw attention to himself and have the teacher involved in mediation, preferring to learn how to handle these situations himself, since they frequently happened on the playground outside of the teacher's purview.

At home he was revered like a "prince" by the grandparents, yet with his parents, he felt unable to meet their expectations much of the time. His nightmare about his "treasures" being taken was profound, as well as his distress in trying to find his parents but becoming "lost in the forest." How could he connect with them? How could he connect with the other children in his classroom? He was looking for a way to have some power, riding a shark bike, but he lacked the resources that are valued in both American society and in his South Asian culture: excellence in academics or sports. He perceived himself as an outsider. To illustrate, I would like to share his first sandplay which often exemplifies the problem.

While he played in the sand, he told a story about a wrestler who wins "everything" (Figures 1 and 2). He displayed great dexterity with the figure and said he "never has to sleep". The wrestler lives in his own house, like a tree house, and has a father who lives in the other tray (not represented) and when the father becomes sad, he comes to visit him, however Anand later changed this to: he has no mother or father and lives with the wrestling team. He told me the wrestler likes to be messy and that he could not be messy at his house.

Here we see Anand's need for power represented by the white muscular man who can live independently and even needs no sleep, who has unlimited powers and does not know defeat. This figure and his story were compensating for Anand's feelings of being an outcast, a loser who was bullied by others and had no power. Anand felt alone and an orphan, with the potential for growth and new beginnings warring with the potential for remaining isolated and on the outside.[29] We know we are on an extraordinary adventure when the orphan archetype is present.

While Anand's parents and grandparents came from a different culture, they also were playing out a dominant American theme, of immigrants without wealth, coming to a new country as laborers and through education of their children hoping to have a better position in the society. This compensation had been ongoing in the family for at least two generations. Anand's self-deprecation, feeling different and rejected, needed to be integrated to lessen his inner critic. Knowing his deficits from the evaluations helped me to help him understand and acknowledge his strengths and to reframe his weaknesses for the parents and to know his gifts.

My efforts were intermittently challenged by his mother who continued to want to find "the cure." At times I felt inadequate to meet her needs, which I am sure was how Anand often experienced his mother. Understanding my countertransference helped to inform me I was on the right track as I worked to help Anand increase his self-esteem so that he could share his feelings with her and others. I also battled the cultural complex of the "Other," as this immigrant family, trying to integrate into "American" culture, faced the difficulty of feeling "Othered" by their son who did not fit in easily.

In all, Anand made 31 trays. At first, Anand always needed to win. His early sandtrays involved battles where his figures always won. Over time, he became more tolerant of allowing the other side to try strategies that might challenge his figures, but he learned strategies to avoid being overtaken. His developing these strategies became a metaphor for his gaining a self-protective stance against the bullying and criticism of others. He became less apt to engage defensively with the bullies, thus becoming less a target for their tactics. He also could seek help when his strategies did not work for him. His emotional flexibility increased.

---

[29] A. Punnett, *The Orphan: A Journey to Wholeness.*

An activity that served as a symbol for his growing flexibility and developing self-protective strategies was his making of a shield. This

**Figure 1. First sandplay** (Photograph: A Punnett, July 2008)

**Figure 2. Close-up, first sandplay** (Photograph: A Punnett, July 2008)

activity followed several months where Anand complained of peers teasing him and now, he was physically retaliating; he was frustrated with how to handle his feelings of anger toward them and of feeling different. He showed an interest in the playroom nerf swords and wanted to engage in play with me using them. He was quite aggressive in the play, and I noted to myself that he was becoming stronger at age 12; his aggression was intense. I decided I needed protection. Providing protection for myself by making a shield could become a model for his gaining protection for himself.

He made the shield over six sessions, which also challenged his ability to stay focused and used his creative energies (Figure 3). In addition, his shield served as a metaphor because the shield symbolizes both defense and attack. He became easily frustrated with the project at times, but we broke this project down into doable blocks of time during each session. He was very enthusiastic about this project and one can see his proud stance with the finished shield.

As Anand made his shield, and I, too, made a shield, I modeled a way of safely fighting. And honestly, I made my shield out of sheer protection! I pointed out he was becoming stronger and needed to know how to handle his male impulses that could hurt someone physically. This activity also served to contain and highlight his challenges from the "Other"—his fight against the "White" culture he experienced and his feelings of being on the outside. He proudly displayed his shield to his parents at one session. This symbolic project became internalized as his personal strength and resolve. As we engaged in these battles, I wondered about the struggles from each of our heritages that were engaged in finding another resolution to the conflicts that existed archetypally. At the same time, I trusted that these struggles were being worked out symbolically.

As Anand improved and physically matured, he became more coordinated and participated on a soccer team and martial arts classes. His grades improved, but he continued to have difficulty with follow-through. In part this difficulty was due to the culture of the family, who intermittently continued to do things for him and did not hold him accountable for his

**Figure 3. Anand with shield he made and sword**
(Photograph: A Punnett, January 2016)

forgetfulness or utilizing strategies he had learned. I reminded Anand's
parents that in the long run, rescuing him did not improve his self-esteem.

His parents were contained in the therapy and were able to access
insights to improving their parenting. For example, Anand's mother
realized she was working against the therapy by yelling and putting him
down. His father began to understand the importance of spending time
with his son, such that he began taking him to work with him during
school vacations or occasionally on weekends. In addition, Anand's father
would take him to religious ceremonies over which they bonded, and
Anand become increasingly proud of his heritage. One could see his
movement from leaving the mother realm to entering the patriarchy as
he identified more and more with his father. Anand was coming more
to accept himself and his heritage such that being different no longer
held the valence of being an outcast.

At the time of discharge, he was now entering middle school, and had achieved much progress academically and physically. His parents would be taking him off his medication over the summer and then seeing how he did once school began. Anand's parents were more enlightened about their parenting and were becoming more supportive of each other as well as having time for each other. However, both acknowledged the difficulties with the trigenerational family living arrangements, but felt they were managing this much better. During our last session, Anand wanted to discuss his progress. He recalled many memories of our times together and his progress over the eight years.

## Concluding Remarks

The United States of America was founded on the principle that all men are created equal, but it has always carried the shadow of superiority, that others, especially non-Europeans or those with darker skin, are less equal than "white" European-Americans. The United States was founded by European-American "white" immigrants. However, the United States will soon be a 'majority-minority" nation, where people of darker skin and/or non-Europeans will be the majority of the population. In addition to these "Others," women, even as the majority, continue to face significant discrimination, as do those who are perceived as non-heterosexual or transgender. Those who were considered Other have been enslaved, incarcerated, tortured, or killed over the years and continue to suffer serious discrimination today. One manifestation of this discrimination is the alarming rate of bullying in the schools, such that there are now zero-tolerance rules against bullying.

While human rights are fundamental to the United States of America, we in the United States continue to struggle with a significant archetypal desire for power and control. America adheres to the racial complex of superiority over minority populations, initially over Africans who were brought here and enslaved, and over Native Americans, and subsequently over all other groups, including all Asians, viewed as darker-skinned. This complex of superiority is gradually changing as more awareness is brought to consciousness regarding this complex.

Family structure and function have changed over the years since the founding of this country; there are more single parents raising children, and of those co-parenting more child and home duties are being shared. Nevertheless, childcare availability has not kept up. Until very recently, the United States had no mandated paid parental leave policy and at this time, it applies only to federal employees.

I presented the case of a boy in an immigrant family who experienced an inner sense of alienation and lacked a sense of belonging in his school community. His family had repeatedly endured the racial complex of the Other, resulting, for both the parents and the child, in feelings of isolation and rejection and not being fully accepted into the community. When I met the family, I was especially moved by their struggle, because of my own family's connection to their country of origin and by my awareness of the oppression endured by members of their culture as a result of "white" rule. Although I will never know what role my grandfather may have played in this oppression, I felt I was repairing something deep within me as I worked with this family.

Through our work together, Anand's parents were better able to accept and parent their son and be more emotionally present and patient with him. He was able to gain the ego strength needed to withstand the experience of being the "Other" and come to accept and integrate more of his family culture. In addition, I saw two archetypes activated within Anand: the orphan, the boy who felt so alone, to the warrior, who confronted his fears and learned to relate to the "Other" as he, a dark-skinned boy raised with the cultural values of his South Asian family, and I, a fair-skinned woman from the dominant American culture, formed our relationship, over our eight years together.

For me "...the process of coming to terms with the Other..." was an important aspect of this therapy "...because in this way we become acquainted with aspects of our nature."[30] Through working with Anand and his family, I became in touch with a possible healing of my family's transgressions against the people from their country. I had not been aware of this before.

---

[30] Jung, *Mysterium Coniuntionis*, CW 14, ¶ 706.

To enter into relationship and to know oneself is the key to all healing. As a Jungian analyst, I benefitted greatly by acknowledging how the cultural complex of the "Other" in American society would influence my work with Anand and his parents. In addition, I was touched by the archetypal energy of working with the Other and perhaps repairing something that went unspoken in our relationship, because of our cultural differences. My hope is that through this work, one by one, family by family, I can help make this United States a country for you and me

## REFERENCES

Anderson, J, Gates, H.L., Kunhardt, P. & McGee, D. (Executive Producers). *The African Americans: Many Rivers to Cross, with Henry Louis Gates, Jr.* (2013, PBS.org.) DVD, 6 hours.

Brewster, F. *The Racial Complex: A Jungian Perspective on Culture and Race.* London, UK & New York, NY: Routledge, 2020.

Bright Hub Education, How World War II Led Women to Enter the Workforce, November 5, 2010, accessed September 6, 2021. https://www.brighthubeducation.com/history-homework-help/94437-world-war-ii-women-in-the-workforce/

Burton, J., Farrell, M., Lord, F. & Lord, R. A Brief History of Japanese American Relocation during World War II, excerpts from *Confinement and Ethnicity: An Overview of World War II Japanese American Relocation Sites,* accessed September 4, 2021, National Park Service. https://www.nps.gov/articles/historyinternment.htm

De Mause, L. (Ed.). *The History of Childhood.* New York, NY: The Psychology Press, 1974.

Flavin, F. Native Americans and American History, University of Texas at Dallas, accessed September 21, 2021. https://www.nps.gov/parkhistory/resedu/native_americans.pdf#:~:-text=Francis%20Flavin%20is%20a%20visiting%20assistant%20professor%20at,and%20the%20history%20of%20early%20and%20nineteenth-century%20America.https://www.nps.gov/parkhistory/resedu/native_americans.pdf

Garcia, E. Schools are still segregated, and black children are paying the price, Economic Policy Institute, February 12, 2020, accessed November 7, 2021.
https://www.epi.org/publication/
schools-are-still-segregated-and-black-children-are-paying-a-price/

Guthrie, W. *This Land is Your Land*, The Asch Recordings, Vol 1, February 18, 1997.

Habenstein, R. & Olson, R.A. Families and Children in History, In C.E. Walker & M.C. Roberts (Eds.), *Handbook of Clinical Child Psychology*. New York, NY: John Wiley & Sons, 1992.

Hilde Kirsch Children's Center, Jung Institute Los Angeles, accessed September 1, 2021. https://junginla.org/clinical-services/
hilde-kirsch-childrens-center/

Johnson, S.N. Stracker News, March 2, 2021, Here's How Much Parental Leave You Get in Every U.S. State. *Newsweek*, September 6, 2021, accessed September 7, 2021.

Jung, C.G. *The Collected Works, Second Edition*. (Bollingen Series XX; H Read, M. Fordham, & G. Adler, Eds.; R.C.F. Hull, Trans.). Princeton, NJ: Princeton University Press, 1953-1979.

——*Two Essays on Analytical Psychology, The Collected Works, Vol.7, Second Edition. (Bollingen Series XX)*. Princeton, NJ: Princeton University Press, 1928.

Leahy, M. Jung and the Post-Jungians on the Theory of Jungian Child Analysis. In A. Punnett (Ed.) *Jungian Child Analysis*. Sheridan, WY: Fisher King Press, 2018.

Mead, S. Child Care Laggard, *U.S. News and World Report*, February 23, 2017, accessed September 6, 2021. https://www.usnews.com/opinion/
knowledge-bank/articles/2017-02-23/the-us-is-a-laggard-on-child-care

Naifeh, K. Encountering the Other: The White Shadow. *Jung Journal: Culture & Psyche*, *13*, 2, 2019.

National Archives, America's Founding Documents, Declaration of Independence Transcript, accessed August 29, 2021.
https://www.archives.gov/founding-docs/declaration-transcript

Pauls, E.P. American Indian, *Encyclopedia Britannica*, accessed September 2, 2021. https://www.britannica.com/topic/American-Indian

Parent. B. What is the Quote on the Statue of Liberty?, accessed September 4, 2021. https://quotes.yourdictionary.com/articles/quote-on-statue-of-liberty.html

Plumer, B. Five Shocking Facts About Child Care in the United States, *The Washington Post*, April 15, 2013, accessed September 6, 2021. https://www.washingtonpost.com/news/wonk/wp/2013/04/15/five-shocking-facts-about-child-care-in-the-united-states/

Punnett, A. *The Orphan: A Journey to Wholeness.* Sheridan, WY: Fisher King Press, 2014.

Roy, M. When a Religious Archetype Becomes a Cultural Complex: Puritanism in America, In T. Singer & S. L. Kimbles (Eds.), *The Cultural Complex: Contemporary Jungian Perspectives on Psyche and Society*. New York, NY: Brunner-Routledge, 2004.

Women's Health Policy: Paid Family and Sick Leave in the U.S., December 14, 2020, accessed September 6, 2021. https://www.kff.org/womens-health-policy/fact-sheet/paid-family-leave-and-sick-days-in-the-u-s/

Yellen, J. L. The History of Women's Work and Wages and How it Has Created Success for Us All, May 2020. Original speech delivered on May 7, 2017 at the "125 Years of Women at Brown Conference", Brown University, Providence RI, accessed September 6, 2021. https://www.brookings.edu/essay/the-history-of-womens-work-and-wages-and-how-it-has-created-success-for-us-all/

CHAPTER 4

# The Children of the Children of Collective Trauma

## Lavinia Țânculescu-Popa
### Bucharest, Romania

## Introduction

Trauma becomes worse because it might not only be misunderstood by other people but also pass for normality. It also creates in the people who experience it a desire to end not only every pain they are living but also any future pain they might experience. There is more than one family who says they do not wish to bring into this world a child who would only suffer. There are many generations who seem to hate the thought of bringing new life into the world under these circumstances. Where there is a lot of pain, new life seems to cease to want to exist. It is there that wounds and suffering need to be alleviated first: there is no place or time for anything else. Everything seems to bode ill and to be diffuse, hard to quantify or to put in words when it is about things that were difficult to express and are still impossible to express and that seem to be circumvented by time or space, as was the case of the unimaginable atrocities in the Nazi labor camps. Both determinate trauma of a definite time (1940-1945) and the cumulative trauma of the general atmosphere of a totalitarian regime such as the Communist one (1945-1990) will continue to transmit transgenerational echoes. This is the backdrop of what existed in Romania.

Just as with the second and third generation of Holocaust survivors, so do the children of contemporary Romania have to bear the shadow of collective trauma and to find their way to step out of it. If this trauma is not understood, for generations to come there will be no future.[1]

> Under Communism, trauma can be understood as a situation in which the victimizers are fellow human beings, justified by law and against whom there is no possibility of reaction...and where the victims are constant witnesses of torture and killings; the loss of human rights and property is total; the extreme situation has no temporal limit."[2]

A void is created, a void explained by Connolly as a "rupture at the heart of the psyche...in which any representation of the experience becomes impossible due to 'the collapse of the imaginative capacity to visualize atrocity.'"[3,4] But not only that: an immense silence that accompanies apparent numbness. Apparent, because underneath it boils fury, anger, disgust. And an immense need to get revenge. But all these feelings are extremely disconnected from the individual capacity of acting, all repressed. Younger people thinking that not they, but their parents were the actual-victims, the actual witnesses of the atrocities of the Communist regime.

### The Family
Communism, with its many facets, one more horrible than another with respect to one's freedom of self-expression, managed to turn men into puppets and women into authoritarian dictators in their homes and about their children's destinies. Both turned this way in order to survive. Both had to swallow a bitter cup of obedience to a totalitarian system in which, if they wanted to survive, they had to learn how to keep silent and obey.

---

[1] O.E. Mill. Stepping Out of the Shadows: Second Generation Holocaust Representation, English Honors Thesis, 31.

[2] A. Connolly. Healing the Wounds of our Fathers: Intergenerational Trauma, Memory, Symbolization and Narrative. *Journal of Analytical Psychology*, 608.

[3] Connolly, 608.

[4] D. Laub & N.C. Auerhahn. Knowing and Not Knowing Massive Psychic Trauma: Forms of Traumatic Memory. *International Journal of Psycho-Analysis*, 288.

In the face of such a power-controlled system one's individual power paled, was silenced. However, inside the individual, there was a turmoil of fury and desire for revenge. This total suppression of the freedom of speech, of opinion, of one's identity was what caused a transgenerational transmission of this trauma of deprivation to the children of the victims of this system, but, even more so, to the children of these children.

Communism never had a humane face. Only a silent, hidden face. You were not allowed to have any authority to look up to, except to the Communist Party. Any attempt to be an individual was terminated. Communism was the great leveler; we were all equal as long as we did not oppose the system in any way. We unequivocally belonged to an amorphous mass, like a great Ouroboric ocean, a Great Mother that forced you to daily swallow your words. The system as a Great Devouring Mother was controlled, at least at first sight, by "Our Beloved Father," comrade Nicolae Ceaușescu. Depicted in drawings of the time as an ideal man, he was, in fact, the first individual absorbed by the system. Extremely weak himself and under constant threat of a negative maternal complex, Nicolae Ceaușescu was the puppet of many strings. The first and most constant, apart from his own inferiority complex's, were the strings pulled by his life companion, comrade Elena Ceaușescu, the symbol of an imposed, "ideal mother." Ceaușescu managed to fake a few ideal images borrowed from his interaction with the great powers. One of his dearest wishes was not to owe anybody anything (while in fact he was a vassal to Russia).

On his death, in 1989, Romania was the only country in the world that had zero external debt and credit of over 2.5 billion dollars. "12-14 April 1989 are days marking...a total economical and political independence of Romania.... For the first time in its long history, Romania is debt free, does not pay tribute to any other country and is truly and completely independent both economically and politically!"[5]

But how was one to realize that in fact Ceaușescu had been a weak individual, who had at one point succumbed to narcissism and was

---

[5] N. Ceaușescu. *Cuvintare la Plenara Mare Comitetului Central al Partidului Comunist Român,* 5.

consumed by an unfathomable delirium of grandeur? He thought of himself as having the right to impart life or death to others. He had become the system. His image was reinforced by the collective shadow of the great powers (Russia, China) which, until recently, had been sub-jugating him. At least unconsciously, or indirectly or obligatorily. For the terror had not been experienced only inside the gulag of the Soviets, but in all the territories that were to be under Russian "guidance" after the Molotov–Ribbentrop pact.

How could one escape the shadow of a mighty oak where not even the grass doth grow but by resorting to grandiose gestures which would, unconsciously, aim at going beyond the majesty of said oak?

## Additional Trauma

The completion of the Lenin Volga-Don Canal, where 900,000 people worked, was outclassed by the completion of the Danube-Black Sea Canal, started by Ceaușescu in 1984, the third largest canal in the world after the Suez and the Panama Canals.[6] This Canal, a gulag in itself, a Romanian concentration camp, leveled any difference between political convicts, non-conformist intellectuals or all other unfortunates who had not realized that a primitive totalitarian system such as the Romanian Communist one would swallow one if one did not obey. Officially, only 656 people died there. But no one knows, in reality, how many people died in that extermination camp, for silence reigned over it, together with millions of square meters of earth, rock and water, covering the bodies that were being transported by trucks and thrown between the banks of the canal to be forever forgotten there.

The same silence surrounded the suffering that was part of the second architectural colossus in the world: the People's House, started in 1984. Ceaușescu was not content with the highest building in Bucharest, Casa Scânteii, a building that imitates one of the stateliest buildings of Moscow (the Lomonosov University). He ordered the building of the People's

---

[6] C. Katona & A. Toma. *The Cargo Evolution Transportation on Romanian Waterways Cernavodă – Agigea and Poarta Albă – Midia Năvodari*, 49.

House, the heaviest building in the world and the second largest one, after the Pentagon. A means of compensating for his weak self. A desire to surpass his authoritative parent (The Great Soviet Union), but not by directly engaging them, rather by implicitly and unquestioningly allowing thousands of lives to be disrupted or lost. As many as 50,000 people were uprooted to clear land for this project. This displacement came against the background of the March, 1977 earthquake in Bucharest which killed over 1500 people and left 35,000 people homeless. Over 20,000 people contributed to erecting the House of the People and no one speaks of the number of the dead buried beneath the scaffolding and the tons of cement. The same deadly silence reigns over their passing.

It took many years for this silence to become all-encompassing. It was accomplished by what was called the re-education of Romania. Re-education was meant to cram in the same  Procrustean bed (the Communist doctrine) all who were openly or indirectly against the Communist regime. These persons lost their right to identity and became "hostile elements," "unsound elements," "isolated elements." "Elements" (objects), not "persons" (subjects).

Communist prisons detained thousands of people who had been condemned for adhering to a different truth. Torture and beatings during investigations were common practices, together with fake trials and "an infernal atmosphere, where you could not sleep a wink for the screams of women that were being beaten up, questioned, the shrieks of those who were being tortured, the moans of those brought back into their cells, black and blue, their feet shattered."[7]

The Ceauşescu regime attacked not just the physical integrity of people, but also their identity, their individual values, their education, their religion and their social values, in general and within their families.

### Education

The educational system was politicized, subject matter that would have endangered the Communist indoctrination and the possibility to find

---

[7] M. Stănescu. *Reeducarea în România Comunistă, Vol. I*, Editura Polirom, Iaşi, 45.

other answers regarding the meaning of one's being was eliminated. Religion was ousted from schools. Faculties, such as Psychology and Educational Sciences, were eliminated. The Faculty of Philosophy, in danger of being dissolved, was integrated into the Party system and only taught ideologies related to Marxism-Leninism and barely mentioned philosophers such as Socrates or Nietzsche. Cultural products were carefully screened before being made available to the public. One of the main weak points of the Romanian education system was that teachers would teach but never educate. A related weakness was that there were no personalized models of teaching: everyone had to be treated the same. Yet not everyone had access to all forms of education. If one's parent was not a Party member, one could not do a Ph.D. However, if the parent was a Party member, one could not study Theology, since a Communist's child could not adhere to such a primitive practice as religion.

### Religion and Morality

One's connection with God was completely severed by the Communist doctrine. This way, one lived alienated from himself or herself. The only supreme authority that he or she could depend on (or was advised to depend on) was the Communist Party. In 1959 came the 410 Decree, which shut down all the monasteries of Romania. The measure was based on the fact that monasteries might be a political danger as they might aid the anti-Communist resistance movement, and harbor insurgents. They were also a spiritual danger, since they might help people preserve their authentic beliefs, their faith, which was unacceptable to an atheist political regime.

People were not only alienated spiritually. Lacking an alive connection with one's spirituality, one's moral side can also be seriously damaged. In this way, reflecting upon one's shadow would be a very difficult if not almost impossible endeavor. "The shadow is a moral problem that challenges the whole ego-personality, for no one can become conscious of the shadow without considerable moral effort. To become conscious of it involves recognizing the dark aspects of the personality as present and real. This act is the essential condition for any kind of self-knowledge."[8]

---

[8] C.G. Jung. *Aion*, ¶ 14.

But how could anyone whose roots are almost taken out, individually and collectively, be able to easily access self-knowledge? Many people were physically uprooted from their birth places (villages in the countryside) and taken to the cities by being reassigned there. This transfer was a dream beautifully sold to these people, as an upgrade in their destiny. Yet it splintered their identity, since they were no longer peasants (for they no longer lived in villages) but they were not city folk either (since they could not properly identify with the city nor were they accepted as belonging there by the city folk). These people would return to their birth places on Saturdays or Sundays to help their parents complete the work in the fields and around their farms. Consequently, their family was not complete either in the city or in the countryside.

## Parenthood

The Ceaușescu regime was intent on regulating family: marriage, preserving marriage and producing children. Unmarried persons were supposed to pay additional taxes; these persons were also criticized during party meetings if they did not marry by a certain age. Divorce was frowned upon and a divorcée was likely to be blacklisted and become a genuine social outcast. 1966 marked the moment of the famous Decree 770 which started the pro-natalist policy in Romania as well as an innumerable string of deviations from the normalcy of parenthood. Claiming that it would protect women's health and, more importantly, the idealized image of the Female Mother, by outlawing abortion, this decree was to open a veritable Pandora's box with devastating consequences: thousands of women were to lose their lives by resorting to non-medical strategies of terminating their pregnancies, assisted or unassisted by medical staff. Hospitals managed to secretly treat women with post-abortion sepsis and many of these interventions did not end well. Language was devised so that it all boiled down to being a woman's issue, not a man's, not a couple's, not a family's. As Luigi Zoja notices, "...as in animal society, the child was entirely the concern of its mother."[9]

It was the woman who got all the blame, she was the irresponsible party, she was supposed to take care not to become pregnant if she did

---

[9] L. Zoja. *The Father: Historical, Psychological, and Cultural Perspectives,* 224.

not want children. And if she fell pregnant and managed to give birth, she was due back to work as soon as possible. The child was left in the care of grandparents (more often than not living precariously in the countryside). If there were no convenient grandparents, the child was taken to daycare (at best) or to a boarding facility for infants. When no other possibilities existed, nor any kind of love on the part of the parents, children were left in the care of orphanages. Here a member of the staff had as many as 30-40 children in their care. Some of these children, manifesting the natural aggression of a child who suffered multiple deprivations, including severe lack of affection, ended up being tied to their beds in order to prevent them from harming themselves.

More bad news was to come. 15,000 of these children became HIV-infected. Uncontrolled blood transfusions caused parenteral infections and were done extensively in the 1980's and 1990's as a method of "infusing the infants with vitamins" and of reducing infant deaths. Sterilizing syringes through boiling was a difficult thing to do since there were shortages of gas, while disposable syringes were a luxury.

A lot of effort was made for the infected children to be kept alive until antiretroviral treatment was made available globally, after 1996. Romania was helped by the World Health Organization, by other countries and by private persons to implement this treatment extensively. Because of this aid, at present, half of these children are still alive. They form the so-called "pediatric cohort" of HIV-positive cases and are registered with the hospitals of infectious diseases of Romania. However, they suffer from multiple medical complications as well as the psychological stigma of rejection from their peers. Even today, Romanian society is prejudiced against accepting HIV-positive persons. These children had a hard time being accepted in schools. Frequently, the parents of their schoolmates demonstrated outside the school buildings demanding that these children be removed from their classes. As adults, they have trouble finding jobs and lose their job if their boss finds out what disease they suffer from. This is why many of them prefer to hide their diagnosis.

Finding a life mate is also very difficult. Some have managed to have families with partners who are also seropositive. By following medical protocols, they give birth to healthy babies and have a pseudo-normal life. Others, unfortunately, prefer to keep their problems to themselves, even hiding their disease from doctors or from their sex partners and thus often infecting many other persons. I learned these facts from a doctor who preferred to preserve his anonymity, following a code of silence that continues to govern such matters.

In Romania, there was then, and even now, an almost total lack of sex education. For many Romanians this is still a taboo subject. Many men had almost no clue about female anatomy and physiology, whereas the idea of prophylactics or any other forms of contraception was only a far-fetched, almost illicit, idea. Menstruation was a subject very rarely broached between daughters and mothers. Girls found out about it from other girlfriends. It was, officially, a sort of collective silence about almost all subjects that had nothing to do with the Party or the five-year plan, doubled by the fact of constant surveillance of people.

## Generational Transmission

The fake patriarch replaced real patriarchs, the real fathers in people's families, who used to possess fortunes during the period between wars, who used to raise as many as eight children themselves and who had tended to farms that had hundreds of cattle before their property had been nationalized by the state. Some of these people (bourgeois/kulaks) were sent to the Canal, their fortunes confiscated in 1947 or turned to ashes when the monetary reform in 1952 took place. As the concepts of property and community were being annihilated, so was the father figure in Romania. Fathers were no longer fathers, as they could no longer offer direction and protection—they could no longer save their children. They were completely alienated from a sense of duty and were slowly becoming useless.

There came a time when everybody would steal from the state's property or from the community ("you were a sucker if you did not leave with at least one brick from your factory to take back home at the end of the workday"), as a passive-aggressive gesture directed towards the veiled aggressor they were dealing with. Everybody "got by." People tried to avoid assuming any kind of responsibility. Although the concept of collectivity existed, the feeling of community was completely missing. Anyone, including the person you shared your life with, could be an agent of the Secret Police. *Divide et impera.*

The second generation turned out to be a generation of people forced and crammed into the boundaries of an undifferentiated crowd. A generation that the system tried to stultify, to turn into a dull mass, without willpower, without initiative or bravery, a generation that would speak in whispers, that was constantly spied upon and that could not express themselves aloud or listen to others voicing their opinions unless they declared themselves as illegal operators, unless they risked being annihilated.

This was a generation starved both physically and informationally. The resources had mostly been regulated in the country (i.e., electricity, gas, etc.). So had food and information. One was allowed a two-hour interval of TV programs, half a loaf of bread a day, three eggs a month. On Christmas, one of the parents would receive one banana or one orange for each child they had. Every evening, usually after 8 p.m., electricity was cut off. Hot water was available only every other day, if you were lucky enough to live in a good area of the city. You could drive your car every other weekend, according to your registration number. Food was always scarce.

The children of the 1970's and the 1980's (the third generation, whom we could call the children of Communism, of the Golden Epoch, or, as some parents called them, "Ceaușescu's children," for most of them were born after the Decree of 1966, not as a result of family planning) thought it a natural thing to hungrily watch green bananas rolled in newspaper slowly ripening on the cupboard, between Christmas and New Year's Eve. They understood that privations were a real thing. They could see their parents struggling against this reality every day. They could understand something of what was going on. They could see the huge lines for food in the small hours of the morning (3-4 a.m.), for they would take turns queuing up for food with their parents. They bore this trauma too, only they had a hard time explaining it.

Their fury and desire for revenge continued to be in the shadows and was unconsciously experienced and repressed as "the power of unconscious influences on human behavior."[10] It somehow got covered by colorful ideals, such as the prized decorative string that indicated your leadership in the classroom or the school you attended or in the camps where you were a Pioneer. Many of these children were innocently convinced that comrade Nicolae Ceaușescu and comrade Elena Ceaușescu were like a second pair of parents, obviously more accomplished and much more powerful than their poor helpless parents at home. It was a matter of pride to see the Ceaușescus being offered wonderful bouquets of flowers by almost perfect-looking children in a country where, if you took more than three carnations to school for your teacher, you could be considered a rich person.

It was also a matter of pride and joy to take part in the parade held on August 23, for which a child would rehearse the whole summer, where they would lift a piece of cardboard or wave a scarf for three minutes. Yes, it was nice to meet your friends during the summer if they did not leave for the seaside or the mountains on vacation with their parents. That was sort of fun. But another sort of fun was for the children of this generation to go on an "agricultural vacation," dan activity based on child labor where children worked in the fields and shared the food packs they received from home. It was like a huge picnic every lunch for two weeks, when learning was not done at school but in the field, where one did not learn about Pythagoras but about good husbandry and about how to unearth potatoes or to husk corn with one's bare hands.

Schools were close to one's home. Children would walk to school. Classrooms seated as many as forty students. Some primary and secondary school teachers would daily discipline their students by applying physical correction. The children did not report them at home. And even if they had, their parents would rarely object or they would have said something like "You deserved it! I told you to apply yourself!" Or, better still, they would apply their own brand of correction to double the one their

---

[10] A. Stevens. *Jungian Approach to Human Aggression with Special Emphasis on War*, 3.

children had already received in class. It was unfair, but the children of Communism considered it a normal thing.

These children are the very parents of nowadays' children and teenagers (the children of the fourth generation). They were the ones who carried on and shared all their contradictory feelings taken from their own parents and amplified them. Fury mingled with nostalgia for that something of Communism that made all of us equal, that helped us not pay for it, not assume anything, not grow either. That terror parents had swallowed inside, that deathly silence about taboo subjects. Those stadiums full of children chanting joyfully and enthusiastically, as in the image that Ceaușescu had appropriated as a result of his visits to China and North Korea in 1971, an image that took his fancy and which he wanted to transfer to the Romanian setting, thus laying one more brick to the foundation of the cult of his personality.

The generation of the children of Communism or the generation of the latch-key children was the most battered one of all. When the Revolution took place, in 1989, they were in primary school, or in high school, or barely starting college. They wanted to see things happening, changing. They did not know what exactly, because they still had some nostalgia for their Pioneer scarves. It was a generation between two worlds. A generation that died for freedom but also the generation that killed the largest number of unborn babies. The first law after the Revolution contained in its first paragraph an abolition of Decree 770. And then, like an almost uncontrolled flood of water, followed the liberalization of so many things. Abortion was one of them. Markets were liberalized, so was information, access to higher education (which until then was often restricted to Party members), access to politics. Industry was liberalized, resources were, too.

But these people, the children of the Golden generation (of Communism) often did not know what to do with freedom. They were, maybe, the most confused group. Some of them did not know what to do, they acted, they lost, they withdrew, they got convinced that freedom of action was not for them. Nor was entrepreneurship. Nor was risk. Nor were riches. They were in full Stockholm syndrome. They got convinced that they needed the same oppressive master their parents had and hated. But there was one thing that they did against this master: they grew up wishing to realize their dreams through their children. For they were still behind psychic bars. The freedom that their brothers had died for in Timişoara, in Braşov, in Bucharest and many other cities of Romania was an ideal become reality but which had gotten devalued as their own strength, courage, self-confidence had trickled away. This battered generation was split between two worlds: the world before and the world after, the world of the reality and of the illusion.

And, as Jung explains, it mostly had to do with "the *'sentiment d'incomplétude'* and the still worse feeling of sterility...explained by projection as the malevolence of the environment, and by means of this vicious circle [where] the isolation is intensified."[11] This was a generation that chose exile to other countries because their own had betrayed them. The Great Mother (Romania) was changing while the Great Father (the regime, Ceauşescu, rules) had disappeared. Out of the blue. Freedom was a joy that the third generation could not partake of. They did not know it so they could not recognize it. Many things are impossible to reconcile in the people of this generation, even thirty years after the Revolution. There still is no father, while the mother still compensates through authority and/or is devoid of femininity.

This third generation, confused and worn-out, transmitted their signals. The children of the current generation (the fourth one, that is) are split between 1) amplifying an idea of freedom both in self-expression and in interpreting the law, the norm, the framework, by creating a lax, responsibility-free atmosphere and 2) adhering undiscriminatingly to the law, in an extremely rigid manner. Both these responses compensate for what happened to the children of the Golden generation.

Currently, we often hear children and teenagers protesting ("It's not fair!" or "I'm bored."), echoing their parents who, in their turn, learnt this from their own parents, who had been silenced, taught to obey and to be passive, in general. Very little of what happened to them was fair.

---

[11] C.G. Jung. *Aion*, ¶ 17.

As for being eternally bored, back then you would have done anything to "do something" in a world in which if a little girl had three dolls of her own she could consider herself rich, happy and even having a duty to give some of her toys away. It is quite clear that the projection of the shadow was carried along more than one generation (three at least), as a powerlessness to express oneself, finally reaching the point in which it has been expelled outwardly. But the psychological context is problematic for these little receivers of their parents' shadow, too.

A meta-analysis of 42 studies on the correlation between the severity of parents' symptoms of posttraumatic stress disorder (PTSD) and children's psychological status underlined that parental PTSD is associated with child distress (anxiety, depression, PTSD and behavioral problems). Also, when both parents are distressed, (as in the situation of the Communist regime that impacted the entire family structure), child functioning could be even more problematic.[12,13]

As Connolly explains, "children of survivors show characteristic deficits such as a failure of metaphorization with subsequent difficulties in distinguishing between reality and fantasy,...which lead to the typical disturbances of memory and of identity."[14] I find it critical to underline this idea of *"disturbances of identity."* For a lot of children from the third generation (the children of Communism), there was rather a confusion in their identity and the way they represented "the adult." Looking at their parents, the ones who should have been their future models, they saw defeated, silenced, weak-willed individuals. At times (when the frustrations, psychological and, maybe, physical pain, became unbearable, such as in the "we have nothing left to lose" state of mind), the same people dropped this cloak and presented themselves as brave, loud, fearless, mostly unconscious of their behavioral impact, so that in the next moment, when a possible unforeseen danger appeared on the horizon, they re-entered their shell of a self-perceived cowardly silence.

---

[12] J.E. Lambert, J. Holzer, & H. Hasbun, 2014.

[13] J.R. Herzog, R. Everson, & D. Whitworth, 2011.

[14] Connolly, 610.

A terrible sense of guilt accompanied not being able to stand up and confront the system. This second generation, confronted with a death of their identity, or rather a premature burying-alive of this sense of identity, could not help transmitting only a partial (if ever) sense of the power of being an adult to their children. Consequently, this unresolved mourning could have led the second generation "to a deficit in the ability to symbolize. These un-metabolized, un-symbolized mental structures are then transmitted to future generations."[15]

In a different manner, the third generation was confused, still challenged, experiencing two regimes, the repression and the paralyzing sense of freedom, exactly in the core of their upbringing (most of them were in their teenage years when the regime switch happened). For them, their childhood was not as bad as later history books were-to say. Still, internally, they inherited some serious deficiencies regarding the sense of identity and how an adult, specifically a parent, behaves.

## Reality in bare painful figures

According to the National Strategy of Parental Education 2018-2025,[16] in Romania these serious problems exist:

1. The rate of infant mortality in Romania, since 1998, continues to be the highest in the European Union: 6.9% in 2016, according to the data offered by the National Institute of Statistics. Malnutrition and premature birth are present as diagnoses leading to mortality.

2. There is a high rate of family abandonment and of children abandoned in hospitals, left without identity papers. In 2013 and in 2014, 1,653 newly born babies were abandoned in maternity wards.

---

[15] C.L. Eizerik. The Past as Resistance, the Past as Constructed. Panel Report. *International Journal of Psychoanalysis*, 388–89.

[16] Romanian Ministry of National Education.

3. Many children have parents who work abroad. At the end of June 2018, the official figures provided by the National Authority for Child Protection and Adoption indicated that there were 94,991 children whose parents were working abroad. Of these, 16,797 were under the care of near or distant relatives without any measures of protection, while the rest had been placed with maternal assistance, placement centers or foster families or persons.

4. A growing number of children were being abused, neglected, or exploited. A UNICEF study in 2015 showed that in Romania, when a child does something wrong, the parents' first response is to raise their voice, whereas 11% parents slap that child or pull their hair.

In addition, not noted in the strategic document quoted above, is a high abortion rate. Official data say that between 1958 and 2018, 22,000,000 abortions occurred,[17] considering that at the beginning of April 2020, Romania had 19,263,080 inhabitants.[18] It is possible that the figures are even bigger, since the statistics do not count the abortions done in private clinics after 1990, medical abortions or abortions performed in the community of Romanians who live abroad.[19]

## Violence of a Thousand Faces

The children of the third generation after the war (the children of the Golden Epoch) faced the silent aggressor in their own parents on the one hand and the seductive ideal parent whom nobody spoke ill of, on the other. These parents, who had learned the tough lesson of utmost obedience, where one did not have a right to appeal, that is, one did not have a right to the words that could help them exist, were brimming with fury. This fury arose from a boundless incapacity for free speech.

---

[17] D. Gheorghe.

[18] Romania Population.

[19] A, Nadane. *Ziarul Lumina* in Sunday Light: Why do I participate in the March for Life?

Even if it is painful to admit, some of these people had a hatred towards the system which was indirectly transmitted to their children through various forms of aggression, whether this aggression was physical or verbal, or both. It was a normal thing for parents to hit their children, as these parents seemed to be incapable of representing in their own minds and in their children's minds the impact of their actions. This habitual, unelaborated aggression swiftly and primitively solved the problem. Then, various forms of verbal aggression would be enacted, regarding the child and the image the child had in the eyes of the parent (*you are a nobody, a fool, a cow, an animal,* etc.), regarding the fact that the child could never become somebody, or by ice cold silence.

This way the silence in which these parents had been forced to exist was transmitted to their children under the form of repeated punishments like "shut up" or "if you say a peep I will knock your teeth out," up to the ice cold silence that defined the atmosphere in which these children were raised and which might have had the most devastating effects on the subsequent manners of their expression. Maybe the most extreme form of aggression, with far-reaching effects, was that some children of the golden generation were never told they were loved or that they had been wanted.

Lacking confidence in their ability to ever surpass their condition as a people whose voices were silenced, the parents of the second generation transmitted to their children a fear combined with a lack of hope, a threat that they would never amount to anything themselves. "You will do no better," "work hard at school and maybe you'll not be a housewife like me," "you'll never amount to anything good," "well, society needs garbage men, too," are the types of expressions that one could often hear in the discourse of a family; they sounded quite normal. This way of expression indicated not just an offensive manner of relating to the child and his or her future but also a form of parental neglect, in which the potential of the child, his/her resources, his/her passions and pleasures were completely overlooked.

In the absence of an acknowledged identity that had been exercised, upheld, developed, these parents might not have had an inner space that they could dedicate to their child. One could argue that the reasons could have a psychological aspect, a logistical aspect or both. Considering the fact that the mothers were to quickly return to work after the birth, that there were extremely few options regarding managing the entire household, that food was scarce and hard to procure, not to mention shortages in electricity, gas, and hot water, the parents (especially the mother) could not attend to the child as much as they would have liked. And, in many cases, the parents were deprived children themselves who did not have the language of love to transmit to their children. Therefore, we see that children of today tend to display "focus on survival issues, lack of emotional resources, and coercion to please the parents and satisfy their needs."[20] They are faced with the contents in their parents' never-metabolized shadow that now possess them and are expressed directly or indirectly in amplified versions. A huge fury buried in a split part of the father, for instance, will generate the need in his boy to fight over and over (apparently with no cause). Actually, the child needs to elaborate the un-elaborated traumatic event that brought his father to split his inner space and to become either extremely powerful or weak. Consequently, he needs to imitate the powerful father in order to separate from the mother. And, in order to gain the strength to liberate from the mother, the boy could identify himself with the aggressor (see the case of James). If the boy fails to separate from the mother because of a weak father model, the child remains in the realm of the Great Mother and becomes passive and submissive. In the case of a girl, when confronted with a very powerful, not elaborated content in the father's split part from the shadow, the girl could become seductive and aggressive in order to attract and destroy the other (see the case of Beatrice) or depressive, if the father is passive and she remains in the realm of the Great Mother (see dozens of other cases in Romanian society, currently).

A space is necessary in the parent to represent and imagine what their child's present needs are and what their child could become. And, in most cases, the child became what the parent decided. This may be a

---

[20] M. Scharf, & O. Mayseless. Disorganizing Experiences in Second- and Third-Generation Holocaust Survivors. 1539.

part of the reason why parents of the fourth-generation children (that is, those children whose self was not strengthened through questions such as "what do you like?") seem to behave overly humbly, in a detached, confused manner when they are supposed to make a decision and act on it themselves. In these adults, one could see the major impact of the authoritarian-paternalistic culture with which they had been accustomed from their grandparents, via their parents.

As there is a deprivation in the sense of identity, there is confusion regarding the act of aggression, in the sense that the parents do not admit that certain acts they perform might be aggressive. They consider some gestures unimportant to mention during an anamnesis or they consider them natural acts. These parents complain of manifest aggression on the part of their child even if, through a trauma transfer, it is they who are the unconscious aggressors. But, as Stevens explains: "One's shadow is a painful and potentially terrifying experience-so much so that we usually protect ourselves from such disturbing awareness by making use of ego-defense mechanisms: we deny the existence of our shadow and project it onto others. This is done not as a conscious act of will but unconsciously as an act of ego-preservation. In this way we deny our own "badness" and project it onto others, whom we then hold responsible for it."[21]

## The Therapy

I would like to illustrate, in this chapter, the situation we are dealing with regarding some families who do not report, for all their sincerity and good will, anything else but aggression on the part of their children, at the beginning of therapy. As a therapist, I ask them questions and the parents have trouble admitting that their own behavior might be aggressive behavior. I will briefly present two case studies in which transgenerational trauma creates in the parents a split and all unbearable content is placed in the split, non-elaborated part, while their Ego is not (apparently) affected, the parents considering all their behaviors to be in the normal

---

[21] A. Stevens, 8.

range of behavior. The silence surrounding this lack of elaboration and hidden aggression has taken various forms.

Generally, I see both parents in the first session; normally this session is longer than 50 minutes. Apart from the parents' reasons for bringing the child in to therapy, I run them through the anamnesis not only of the child, but also of the context in which the child came into the world, including quality of the relationship as they assess it, extended family context, marital status, socio-professional aspects (jobs of parents), and logistic aspects (where they live). I do this detailed "interview" so I can clarify possible roots of the child's condition. I have found, in my experience, that if not prompted, the parents do not really know what would be important to mention in relation to the context in which the child is living.

The next encounter would be with the child, during 4-5 sessions. I take notes and reflect upon possible clarification questions to address to the parents. This first set of sessions helps in moving something (of a great or lesser importance in the child) and gives room for discussion in the next encounter with the parents, which happens after these first 4-5 sessions.

This second encounter with the parents is important because the parents have had time to reflect upon some questions addressed in the first session and also upon the observed modifications in the child during this month of process. Normally, this is the moment in which the parents decide whether the child continues the process or not. If the process continues, we run periodic review sessions once every 4-6 months or, at the parents' request, earlier and not too often, so the therapeutic field remains the child's and is not transformed into a couple/family therapy.

CASE 1: BEATRICE

Beatrice (pseudonym) was 4 when her parents brought her to therapy. The parents complained that Beatrice, who had a brother who was 5 years older, was extremely aggressive verbally. She cursed, she used all sorts of bad words, horrible words even for an adult, let alone a four-year-old, she would scream and spit at everybody. Up to the moment she had been brought to therapy, Beatrice had been kicked out of four kindergartens. She was at her fifth. The parents were at their wits end. They promised over and again that they had never hit her, had never used foul words towards her and that no one spoke bad words in their home. The child however used foul language, she could swear vilely, used all sorts of offensive words and insults to her mother, her father, her brother, every acquaintance, or stranger. One day she had even scratched a car with a coin in a moment of fury. The parents were beyond themselves. They could not understand her or stop her.

There followed a relatively short therapy (fewer than ten sessions). I could read aggression in her eyes. It was the kind of a look that one finds in any person spoiling for a fight. She worked with sand, and she constantly threw sand out of the box, against my express wishes, as if she wanted to tell me: "Now, what are you going to do to me?"

On the surface, Beatrice played nicely, she had dolls with nice dresses, ribbons, like any little girl her age. But, from time to time, when I felt things were looking up, she would make an aggressive gesture, looking at me inquisitively, but, in the same time, seductively. I repeated to her my rules and I asked her not to throw the sand out of the box, so that other children could enjoy it later, too. She seemed not to hear me.

During one particular session, things went completely wrong. Only a few minutes after the session started, she went to the toy shelf, put up her hand and suddenly swiped all the toys off the shelf, while eyeing me curiously. Then, she rubbed off her hands like an adult completing an illicit task and said, again, seductively and almost "helplessly heartbroken:" "Oops, they fell!"

I felt helpless. I could feel her pain was so deep that she wanted to test me and see whether I could exist in her pain with her, without judging her. I said I would gather all the toys and put them back after she left, that she could play with something else. Then, I noticed her first sign of empathy, maybe a tinge of pity. She said she would help me gather the toys and so we put the toys back on the shelf together. This *reparatio* we made together must have helped immensely. But it was not sufficient, that was clear.

Later on I touched on the idea of possible early trauma. The parents swore on their lives that, apart from a moment when the child had burnt herself by touching the heated oven, when she was eleven months old and could barely walk, she had never gone through anything bad. However, after some discussion with my supervisor, she came up with an idea. She told me to ask them about how the child was parted with her pacifier. The next time we met, I asked the parents. The mother said triumphantly: "She was already two years old and would not be parted from the thing. So we found an ingenious manner to wean her off: we would daily cut a bit off the pacifier, until there was nothing left. Beatrice tried to suck at it for a while and then we told her it had broken and there was nothing to it. There were no pacifiers left to buy at the store." The mother was very pleased with this strategy without understanding that this had been an unimaginable act of aggression on their part: the slow destruction of the transitional object was equivalent in aggression to the destruction of the mother's replacement object in which Beatrice could trust more than in the "unreal mother devotion and reliability,"[22] as Winnicott explains. From the moment I had this talk with the parents, maybe prompted by shame and maybe a feeling of guilt that they had not realized what they had done, they ceased bringing Beatrice to therapy. Years later, I talked to the mother who told me that Beatrice was doing okay, only she had some trouble with Maths. No wonder: the major difficulty that was still active in Beatrice was her own managing of rules, namely the relation with her absent father during the aggression and at any moment.

## CASE 2: JAMES

When he started therapy, James (pseudonym) was five years old. He had been brought to therapy by his mother who had become very concerned with the fact that James was behaving violently to his little brother, Robert (pseudonym), who was younger by three years. Their mother remembered that ever since the time of her pregnancy, James had been threatening to kill his brother. Since Robert had been born, James had

---

[22] D.W. Winnicott. *Playing and Reality*, 32.

already tried twice to eliminate his brother by pressing a pillow over his face. The parents were horrified not only at these events but also at the fact that whenever he interacted with other children, James showed aggression, looked down on them and beat them up. According to his parents, James was hyperactive at home, exhausting everybody and making them complain of his aggressive behavior (his nanny, his grandparents, other children in the family).

James came from a family that really wanted children and that was trying to ensure a good non-violent upbringing for their children, a secure environment.

I worked well with James, but we stood close, in the dark. I could feel something eluding me, yet I could not tell what. He sometimes played in the sand. Sometimes he played with the toy figures on a table. He drew rarely. Quite rarely. In the sand, with the toys, in his drawings, there were three obstinately recurring themes: struggle and defeat, the double, and an adult rescuing a child. More often than not, these themes or images were hidden or became covered with sand at the end of the session. It was like a silence which he kept drawn over him and would not shed. I respected his wish to keep silent. When he did say something, he very often spoke in metaphors, and I, from the space that I had created for him inside myself, felt that I had to understand him. And I showed him that. He would say "I know you understand" and was content.

It was two years since James had begun therapy. The same struggles, always against somebody, the same moments in which he would say that two knights/soldiers/Tom and Jerry figures were fighting and the one representing him was defeated. I had begun to feel his impatience, his boredom. And, somehow, his inability to have a different reaction. These themes had taken shape within me too, and I could see them clearly. However, I held on, welcoming and remaining curious every time we met. I mirrored him in times he was looking for an answer to his almost rhetorical questions, showing him, not only that someone was there for him, but also that someone understood him. I knew that the answer would come from somewhere.

And one day, we held a special session. He wanted to take all the sand out of the box and put it somewhere else. He put a dolphin in the empty box that no longer held any grain of sand. Then, right in the middle of this session, James asked for pencil and paper and asked me if he could draw something. I told him that he could. He immediately drew a square, a child inside the square, a bulb hanging from the ceiling of the square. He looked at me, and after he made sure that I was there for him, he scratched an x over the bulb. He told me, before I could ask anything (as a matter of fact I keep silent and let the patient say something about the drawing, the image he has produced, the dream): "This is me when Daddy locked me in the bathroom. It was dark and I remained there for a long time." I felt a stab of fear. Everything was quiet. I now understood that the mother (the sand) had left him in that moment and in the endless dark of the sea he was alone, like a dolphin crying.

At the first session I held with the parents after this, I told them that I would like to find out about the episode in which James had been locked in the bathroom. The father said, almost with a smile, that it had happened once when he had been disobedient. It had been a long time ago. I asked the father if the light had been off. He said: "Yes, it was, but he knew we were right behind the door, so I don't think he was frightened." My heart was beating fast. I could understand, by my link with the child, that for a 4 to 5-year-old, one minute was an eternity, let alone two minutes in the dark. It must have been like a murder, an unimaginable act of aggression. I felt deep sadness at the thought that the parents did not understand how aggressive they had been and that there might be other gestures they might inadvertently do to James and even maybe to Robert.

During the next meeting, James placed in the sand a fireman saving a baby. He covered them in sand up to their necks but assured me that he had not covered their mouths and that they could breathe. And that they would turn out fine. There followed a set of sand trays with a mountain that at first had a hole in its top, as if it had been a volcano. The first of these sessions was very painful, full of silence, as if he had recognized his own state of sadness and depression into which he had sunk. The next sand trays contained a mountain decorated with rocks and, at the end, the mountain made room for a small lake around which a witch and a magician would converse on equal footing, while a white horse and a black one were standing by, together with a rowboat. By the final sessions, the witch had been defeated, the magician was caught in the pile of sand and the two horses, as the brightest and the darkest form of energy, worn-out, exhausted but alive, were ready to recover some day, integrated.

## Concluding Remarks

In these two cases, the common element is the fact that, as a therapist, it was essential for me to create an inner space for the child in which he/she could know that he/she has a place to live. This symbolic multidimensional space, this sacred archetypal *temenos*[23] was more than a logistic setting and a therapeutic frame. Of course, the office, the dedicated interval of time for his/her session, the fact that there was an adult always there and waiting for him/her, present, non-judgmental, available inside, offered the child the confidence that he/she matters. Also, it was important to the analytic processes that I imagine that space for the child and tell the child about that space in which he/she felt seen, listened to, secure, and understood.

At times, a positive projective identification encompassed our sessions, compensating for the inverse phenomenon that, as observed also in case of the children of Holocaust survivors, "they become the 'containers' for their parents' projections."[24] Therefore, "the child then starts to think, feel and act in accordance with the projection."[25] The method that I applied was that I communicated to my little patients not only the compassionate feeling in relation to what they might have felt, but also that they might want to consider that their parents (whom the patients often condemned, in a whispered voice) were also in the same position, educated like this, by their parents. I used this method in approaching difficult conflictual situations (in which the parent appeared as the

---

[23] L. J. Ravitz, Child Analysis and the Multilayered Psyche, 37.

[24] D. Rowland-Klein & R. Dunlop. *The Transmission of Trauma Across Generations: Identification with Parental Trauma in Children of Holocaust Survivors*, 367.

[25] T.H. Ogden. *Projective Identification and Psychotherapeutic Technique*, 18.

aggressor), not for justifying in any way the parent's unconscious act of aggression, but rather to give the patients the understanding that they were not the ones to blame, nor the parents the ones to be condemned and to help the children loosen the tension they felt in relation to their parents.

The major difficulty, starting from their family, was to restructure the model of relating to aggression and of giving the child the feeling that he/she could choose in a determinate frame what is particular to him/her, what defines him/her best, without repercussions that might affect him physically or, most importantly, emotionally. And as Punnett points out, one important need is "the need for identifications and then separations from the maternal and paternal complexes to the evolving uniqueness for each child."[26]

Most of the time, born from this collective trauma, a cultural complex emerges. This complex may manifest either in feeling oppressed, weak, ready to complain or waiting forever for help, or, in compensation, by feeling exceptional, proud, fierce, and seeking one's own advantage. Beyond the fact that this non-representation of trauma, of not-elaborated, clustered aggression inside the parent, might seem normal and yet might have a deep impact on the child, the parents should manage to find their own inner spaces and time that they could offer their children. In this way, the children could transpose in this space and time what is reserved to them from within their parents, their unique print which the parents might – fortunately – fall in love with as soon as they have learned it.

Decades beyond the onset of this collective trauma, in countries that lived for generations under the terrors of totalitarian regimes (such as Romania), "a collective personification like the trickster...continues to make its influence felt."[27] And, even if people tried to transform the trickster into the main character of their compensatory jokes (i.e., in jokes about Bulă, a buffoon or coward), where a fool or scapegoat, not them, was to blame, as Jung explains, "part of him gets personalized and is made an object of personal responsibility."[28] When the pain of that

---

[26] A. Punnett. Children's Dreams, 139.

[27] C.G. Jung. *The Archetypes and the Collective Unconscious,* ¶ 468-469.

[28] C.G. Jung. *The Archetypes and the Collective Unconscious,* ¶ 469.

# REFERENCES

Ceaușescu, N. Cuvintare la Plenara Mare Comitetului Central al Partidului Comunist Român, Editura Politică, *București*, 5, 1989.

Connolly, A. Healing the Wounds of our Fathers: Intergenerational Trauma, Memory, Symbolization and Narrative. *Journal of Analytical Psychology*, 56, 5, 607–626, 2011. doi:10.1111/j.1468-5922.2011.01936.x

Eizerik, C.L. The Past as Resistance, the Past as Constructed. Panel Report. *International Journal of Psychoanalysis*, 91, 387–90, 2010.

Gheorghe, D. How Romania came to have 22 million abortions, *România Liberă*, February, 20, 2011, accessed on April 17th, 2020. https://romanialibera.ro/special/reportaje/cum-a-ajuns-romania-sa-aiba-22-milioane-de-avorturi-217321.

Groups of Students Arrested and Convicted Following the 1956 Events [ro: Loturile studenților arestați și condamnați în urma evenimentelor din 1956], *The Truth* [Adevărul], October 28, 2006, accessed on April 17th, 2020, https://adevarul.ro/sanatate/medicina/loturile-studentilor-aresta-ti-condamnati-urma-evenimentelor-1956_50abb5e67c42d5a6637f0bb7/index.html

Herzog, J. R., Everson, R.B. & Whitworth, J.D. Do Secondary Trauma Symptoms in Spouses of Combat-Exposed National Guard Soldiers Mediate Impacts of Soldiers' Trauma Exposure on Their Children? *Child and Adolescent Social Work Journal*, 28, pp. 459–473, 2011. doi:10.1007/s10560-011-0243-z

Jung, C.G. *The Collected Works, Second Edition.* (Bollingen Series XX; H Read, M. Fordham, & G. Adler, Eds.; R.C.F. Hull, Trans.). Princeton, NJ: Princeton University Press, 1953-1979.

------- Aion: Researches into the Phenomenology of the Self. *The Collected Works Vol. 9ii.* (Bollingen Series XX). Princeton, NJ: Princeton University Press, 1978.

-------The Archetypes and the Collective Unconscious. *The Collected Works Vol. 9i.* (Bollingen Series XX). Princeton, NJ: Princeton University Press, 1969.

Katona, C. & Toma, A. The Cargo Evolution Transportation on Romanian Waterways Cernavodă – Agigea and Poarta Albă – Midia Năvodari. "Mircea cel Batran" *Naval Academy Scientific Bulletin*, 13, 1, Constanta, Romania: "Mircea cel Batran" Naval Academy Press, 2015.

Lambert, J.E., Holzer, J. & Hasbun, A. Association Between Parents' PTSD Severity and Children's Psychological Distress: A Meta-Analysis. *Journal of Traumatic Stress*, 27, 9–17, 2014.

Laub, D. & Auerhahn, N.C. Knowing and Not Knowing Massive Psychic Trauma: Forms of Traumatic Memory. *International Journal of Psycho-Analysis*, 74, 2, 287–302, 1993.

Mill, O.E. Stepping Out of the Shadows: Second Generation Holocaust Representation. English Honors Theses. 26, 2017. http://digitalcommons.trinity.edu/eng_honors/26

Nadane, A. *Ziarul Lumina* in Sunday Light: Why do I particpate in the March for Life? *News for Life*, March 17, 2019, accessed on April 17, 2020, https://stiripentruviata.ro/ alexandra-nadane-in-Sunday-light-why-participate-in-the-march-for-life.

Ogden, T.H. *Projective Identification and Psychotherapeutic Technique*. New York, NY: Jason Aronson, 2-18, 1991.

Punnett, A. *Children's Dreams in Jungian Child Analysis* (A. Punnett, Ed.). Sheridan, WY: Fisher King Press, 133–156, 2018.

Ravitz, L. J. Child Analysis and the Multilayered Psyche. In: *Jungian Child Analysis* (A. Punnett, Ed.). Sheridan, WY: Fisher King Press, 21–42, 2018.

Romanian Ministry of National Education, National Strategy for Parental Education 2018-2025, accessed on April 17th, 2020, https://holtis.ro/ proiect-strategia-nationala-de-educatie-parentala-2018-2025

Romania Population. https://www.worldometers.info/world-population/ romania-population/, accessed on April 17th, 2020.

Rowland-Klein, D. & Dunlop, R. The Transmission of Trauma Across Generations: Identification with Parental Trauma in Children of Holocaust Survivors. *Australian and New Zealand Journal of Psychiatry*; 31, 358–369, 1997.

Scharf, M. & Mayseless, O. Disorganizing Experiences in Second and Third-Generation Holocaust Survivors. *Qualitative Health Research*, 21, 11, 1539 – 1553, 2010. doi:10.1177/1049732310393747.

Stănescu, M. Reeducarea în România Comunistă, Vol. I, Editura Polirom, *Iași*, 2010.

Stevens, A. Jungian Approach to Human Aggression with Special Emphasis on War. *Aggressive Behaviour,* 21, 3-11, 1995.

Winnicott, D.W. *Playing and Reality*. London, UK: Routledge, 2005.

Zoja, L. *The Father: Historical, Psychological, and Cultural Perspectives*. London, UK: Brunner-Routledge, 2001.

# CHAPTER 5

# Child Analysis in Taiwan (The Republic of China)

## *Mei-Fang Huang*

### Taipei, Taiwan

## Early Occupations and Settlement

Taiwan, officially, The Republic of China, represents a complex mixture of cultural influences, which will be outlined below. These influences have resulted in the unique culture, collective conscious and unconscious of Taiwan.

### AUSTRONESIAN "ABORIGINAL" SETTLEMENT AND CONTROL FROM 4000 BCE - 1624 CE

Austronesian speakers are the first known settlers of Taiwan, from approximately 4000 BCE. Initially hunters and gatherers and subsequently also farmers, their descendants are known as the "Aboriginal" or "Indigenous" groups of Taiwan.

### DUTCH, SPANISH, MING INFLUENCES, 1624 - 1683

The Dutch and Spanish vied for control of Taiwan in the first half of the 16th century, with the Dutch expelling the Spaniards in 1642. The Dutch encouraged migration of Han Chinese from the mainland, up to 50,000 having arrived by 1661. In 1661, members of the Ming Dynasty, fighting a losing battle against the Qing Dynasty in mainland China, retreated to Taiwan and expelled the Dutch. During the European and Ming occupations, some of the aboriginal groups fell under their control, while others remained independent.

QING DYNASTY CONTROL, 1683 - 1895

In 1683, the Qing Dynasty took control of Taiwan, ruling Taiwan for 212 years, until 1895. Under Qing rule, many Han Chinese, primarily from Fujian Province and also from Guangdong, immigrated to Taiwan. These immigrants came to greatly outnumber the aboriginal groups and earlier Chinese immigrants. For more than two hundred years, Han culture in Taiwan influenced food, clothing, housing, transportation, living habits, religion and literature. As a result, the aboriginal groups on the Taiwan plain were gradually Sinicized and almost disappeared in the early 20th century.

## Japanese Occupation from 1895 to 1945

In 1895, at the conclusion of the first Sino-Japanese War, China and Japan signed the Treaty of Shimonoseki and Taiwan was ceded to Japan. The Japanese occupied Taiwan from 1895 to 1945. At various times during this period, there were uprisings and resistance to Japanese rule. Although all Taiwanese were under strict military control, with deadly consequences if they rebelled, until 1930 the aboriginal population was treated more harshly than the Han Chinese. The "Musha incident," in 1930, in which both Japanese and indigenous people were slaughtered, led to reforms in which the indigenous groups obtained status more equal to those of the Han Chinese, although both groups still suffered under the Japanese.

During the period when Japan occupied Taiwan, it implemented modernization, through railroad construction, sanitation and public health measures, universal primary education and industrialization.

During the Taisho era of Japan (1912 - 1926) new ideas of freedom, democracy and socialism were popular in Taiwan. Moreover, with the trend of national self-determination in the world, the people of Taiwan actively fought for autonomy and in 1935, achieved local autonomy in elections. In this period before World War II, although there was no longer armed resistance to Japan in Taiwan, cultural resistance continued in literature, art, and social cultural movements.

In 1936, Japan once again tightened its grip on Taiwan. It instigated the "Kominka Movement," or the Japanization of Taiwan, through banning the use of Chinese in schools, by insisting that people have Japanese names, and by drafting Taiwanese into the Japanese Imperial Army.

Throughout the Japanese occupation, Japanese culture penetrated the people's lives and became part of Taiwanese culture. However, it is important to remember that important aspects of Japanese culture, such as its written language, descended from Japan's interaction with the Tang Dynasty of China in the 7th - 9th centuries. Hence, Taiwanese already shared common elements in their collective unconscious with their Japanese rulers.

## From 1945 to the Independence of Taiwan

In 1945, World War II ended and Japan was defeated. Taiwan was returned to the Republic of China (ROC) which was governed by the Kuomintang (KMT). The KMT governed mainland China from 1928 until 1949. Since Taiwan identified primarily with the Han culture, most Taiwanese looked forward to becoming part of the Republic of China. However, under Japanese governance, the infrastructure of Taiwan and concepts of modern life had become more advanced than they were in China.

After the second civil war between the Communist Party of China and the Kuomintang in 1949, the People's Republic of China (PRC) was founded in mainland China and the Kuomintang withdrew to Taiwan. Since then, the regime of the Republic of China (ROC) has referred only to the island of Taiwan, the Penghu Islands, the Matsu Islands, and the Kinmen Islands. The retreat of the ROC to Taiwan resulted in a second wave of migration of Han Chinese to Taiwan, estimated to be 1.2 million people. Different from the earlier immigrants, this group included people with different languages, religions and cultures from various parts of China.

The impact of this migration was significant on all aspects of Taiwanese life. In addition, the ROC imposed martial law on Taiwan, from 1945 to 1987. Starting in 1987, Taiwan has transitioned to full democracy and emphasis on Taiwanese, rather than mainland Chinese culture. Significant tensions and conflicts remain with mainland China, however.

**Resistance Movements in Taiwan Under the ROC, 1949 - 1987**
In 1949, when the Kuomintang withdrew to Taiwan, its position was rendered tenuous by the PRC in China. The PRC bombarded the Taiwan Strait from 1949 - 1979. In October, 1971, the United Nations replaced the ROC by the PRC and the ROC subsequently withdrew from the United Nations. On January 1, 1979, U.S. President Jimmy Carter announced the establishment of diplomatic relations with the PRC and broke off diplomatic relations with Taiwan. However, after the U.S. announced the establishment of diplomatic relations with the PRC, the U.S. Congress also passed the Taiwan Relations Act empowering the U.S. government to continue trading, cultural and other relations between the United States and Taiwan. During those years, the political and social climate in Taiwan was turbulent and the people were anxious. However, the ending of official relations between Taiwan and the U.S. actually led to the democratization of Taiwan.

At the time, Taiwanese President Chiang Ching-kuo cancelled the upcoming election of public representatives due to the national crisis. National protests were prohibited. This suppression led to the "Kaohsiung Incident" in 1979, a major suppression of opposition leaders which ultimately led to a move toward democratic reforms. From the middle of the 1980s, following these changes in the situation and the cessation of bombardment from mainland China, people in Taiwan started demanding the termination of martial law which had been enacted in 1949 in response to the perceived threat of the Communist Party of China. This martial law controlled people's rights to assembly, establishment of associations, expression of opinions, publication and travel. Many people were imprisoned, some were executed. This period was known as "The White Terror." Martial law was formally ended in 1987.

**Worries to be Swallowed Up and Isolated**
Due to the historical and cultural factors described above, the Taiwanese people have enduring anxieties. With China on the other side of the Taiwan Strait, the fear of armed attack in Taiwan changes from time to time, but never disappears. Moreover, the climate of international

politics significantly influences the Taiwanese. Using public health as an example, in 2003 during the SARS epidemic, Taiwan could not join the World Health Organization (WHO) due to the obstruction of China. Taiwan could not cooperate with WHO and was prevented from receiving information or data. The same situation has prevailed with the COVID-19 pandemic.

As a small island country, Taiwan must exchange resources and services with other countries. It is also absolutely vulnerable to powerful larger countries. It must apply flexible diplomatic strategies. "People-to-people diplomacy" becomes part of everyone's life. The people fear being swallowed by the great powers or being isolated by powerful countries which cooperate with other countries through threats and incentives of profits. The anxiety continues. In such a situation, survival and striving for independence are common issues experienced by Taiwanese.

## Struggle of Identification

Before the termination of martial law, educational materials in Taiwan were based on ROC government materials before the KMT withdrew to Taiwan, i.e., before 1949. After the ending of martial law in 1987, people could discuss everything about Taiwan, including the culture of indigenous peoples, resistance to and acknowledgment of benefits from Japan, attitudes towards the U.S. and towards the Taiwanese independence movement. They could more openly approach socialism and nationalism and even talk about the 228 Incident of February 28, 1947 when the KMT suppressed Taiwanese nationalists, killing over 5,000 people. At the time, there were serious confrontations between "mainlanders" (Chinese who retreated with the ROC to Taiwan) and the local Taiwanese.

At that time, the Taiwanese questioned "who we are." In terms of consciousness and politics, we were "Taiwanese." Otherwise, the dispute over independence or unification with the ROC had no meaning. Nevertheless, the traditional Chinese characters and language we used were our cultural heritage from the Han people.

In 1960, Taiwan implemented Ten Constructions of Livelihood and Economy. The underlying meaning was that Taiwan changed its political position of "regain the mainland" to establishment as an independent country. After the termination of martial law, educational materials emphasized Taiwanese history as well as linking Taiwanese culture to its historical Han influences. In terms of culture, we were born and raised in Taiwan and we should be "Taiwanese." However, we share a common history with China. We are even proud to be the legitimate inheritors and bearers of Han culture regarding our written and spoken language. However, with the genes of our original Austronesian forebears, we are not pure Han people.

As discussed above, Taiwanese individuals experience various cultural impacts and are confused by "who we are." In terms of consciousness, Taiwanese have a national identity. However, as to the unconscious, there is a crisis of connection between ego and Self.

Because of political oppression and upheaval, our relation with Austronesian culture or pan-Asian continental culture[1] shows unconscious resistance. Due to long-term Han cultural influence, most Taiwanese have only a tenuous connection to Austronesian or Indigenous culture and can only explore, in-depth, unconscious materials from those cultures (such as the myths of Indigenous people). Regarding the association with pan-Asian continental culture, we fear losing our independence with the acquisition of that culture.

## Families in Taiwan

The Chinese value interpersonal relations and family above all. Filial obedience and ethics are the core values in maintaining family relationships. Children should show obedience to their parents, respect all elders and love their siblings. However, in the last hundred years, with the influence of western individualism and social changes, the Taiwanese people's family structure, parenting functions and educational concepts have encountered significant challenges.

---

[1] For the author, "China" and "Han people" cannot represent the countries and nations of "China" in the past 5000 years. Thus, I refer to "Asian continental culture."

FAMILY STRUCTURE

In the last 70 years, family structure in Taiwan has changed significantly. The changes can be seen in the evolution of private housing and the reduction of the birth rate in Taiwan.

Apart from indigenous peoples' housing, traditional private residences in Taiwan followed the model of Chinese compound houses introduced by the first Chinese immigrants in the 17th century. These traditional Chinese residences exemplified social norms, family ethics and attitudes towards the relationship between humans and nature. The houses could be added onto, as children grew up and started their own families. In addition, they had a central space for worship and for family ceremonies.

When the Japanese took control of Taiwan in 1895, the Meiji Restoration occurring in Japan triggered the modernization of Taiwan and resulted in urbanization of Taiwan, including changes to family residences. However, these changes occurred gradually.

Both during the Qing Dynasty and under Japanese rule, many modern public buildings were constructed, such as train stations, government buildings, schools and hospitals. The children of the gentry and land-owners returning to Taiwan after studying in Japan or Europe began constructing western-looking residences. Although these Taiwanese homes were outwardly western, they retained rooms for worshipping the gods and ancestors. The arrangement of the rooms remained based on the traditional concept that "man is superior to woman." Traditional influences of feudal society still existed during the period.

During the 1920s, private residences in Taiwan changed more significantly. The width of the corridors was increased to resist the heat in summer. The windows of main halls and rooms were enlarged. "Bright halls and dim rooms" of traditional private houses no longer existed. Big cooking stoves in the kitchen were reduced and the families were divided into smaller units. The layout of private houses reflected owners' occupations or social status. For instance, doctors, lawyers, and the middle class in the cities added entrance halls, children's rooms, toilets and gardens in the houses. Changes were insignificant in the rural and indigenous areas since those living there believed that traditional housing could satisfy their living needs.

In the 1930s, influenced by the design movement of Modernism in Europe and America, building materials, structures, space and appearance changed even more. The shrines of the ancestors were moved to the corners of the buildings. The spatial layout was freer, and ventilation and lighting of the rooms were valued.

These housing changes reflected underlying cultural changes. At the end of the 19th century, residences revealed the family power distribution of Chinese traditional feudal society. In the early 20th century, residential housing began to show the impact of western and Japanese culture in Taiwan, while many traditional elements and attitudes were maintained. In the 1930s, under the influence of internationalization and modernization, women's status was upgraded and children's living space became valued. More emphasis was placed on smaller family units. However, "familism" in traditional culture was still an invisible presence.

In the last 70 years, the number of family members in Taiwanese families also declined dramatically. When the KMT arrived in Taiwan in 1949 with 1.2 million immigrants with their concept from traditional society, "the more children, the more blessings," the population in Taiwan increased sharply. Afterwards in order to stop the population explosion, the government promoted family planning. In 1967, it proposed "Five Threes:" giving birth three years after marriage, the second birth three years later and the third birth three years after that, three children at most and finishing giving birth before the age of 33. In 1971, family planning was changed to "two children are just right, and boys and girls are both nice." In 2019, according to the government, the birth rate was only 1.050, below replacement rate. In the past, grandparents and parents took care of an average of seven children in the family. Today, grandparents and parents are in charge of one or two children, who become more important.

POWER STRUCTURE WITHIN THE FAMILY

In Chinese traditional society, men were seen as superior to women. In modern times, although women's status has been upgraded, men and boys are still seen as more important. In ancient times, when wives did not bear children, husbands could legitimately marry their concubines. In Han culture, continuing the family line was all-important. Sons inherited the family properties, were expected to take care of the parents, and fulfill family obligations. As adults, women got married and moved to their husband's families.

The centuries' old tradition of "men are superior to women" showed up in many ways. Before the 1980s, a woman would continue giving birth to daughters until she had a son. In the family of the author's high school classmate, there were five girls since the mother had not had a son. Due to her age, she stopped giving birth after having the fifth daughter. In traditional society, women who could not have a son were "useless." Although science has proven that the infant's gender is determined by the father's sperm, the generation of grandparents has rarely accepted this fact.

In traditional culture, where men were superior to women and where there were often many children, most of the resources were invested in the boys. Before the 1960s, girls had to work at an early age and contributed their incomes to the parents to pay for the boys' schooling. Since girls were treated as "money-losing goods" (when the girls grew up and got married, the parents had to prepare dowries), some families sent the girls to be "child brides" to forgo the dowries.

In Taiwan, the tradition of "men are superior to women" has declined with modernization, and families produce fewer children. However, this concept still influences the family power structure in different ways. The first way is in the relationships of the three generations in families.

In modern families, with one or two children, parents tend to treat the boys and girls equally, while grandparents who grew up in the time when men were superior to women prefer boys. Because family relations are important, people are expected to respect older family members who think that their opinions should be valued. Thus, the parents-in-law with whom the mother lives, tend to unconsciously show their preference for boys. Using the author's two good friends as examples, friend A had two sons and her parents-in-law never asked her if she wanted to have another child. Friend B had twin girls and her parents-in-law sometimes asked her if she wanted to have a boy.

In addition, in the families of Taiwan, retired grandparents often take care of the grandchildren for their children. Thus, the grandchildren might recognize "men are superior to women" from their grandparents, even when their parents are more egalitarian towards them.

The genders of the children of the third generation can influence relationships between parents and grandparents, between themselves and grandparents and among the brothers and sisters. While competition among siblings occurs for many reasons in Chinese society, the factors of sibling competition include gender. When the preference of parents or grandparents for the children is determined by gender, the girls see that their parents and grandparents favor the boys and that as girls, they are not treated equally no matter how outstanding they are and they feel frustrated.

PARENTING STYLE

In the 1970s, Taiwan became an industrialized society. The parents of today's children and teenagers were born mostly after the industrialization and urbanization of Taiwan. Although they grew up under the martial law of the ROC, they were strongly influenced by western culture, with its democratic parenting style. However, important aspects of Chinese attitudes towards parenting remain. These include emphasis on "control" and on "filial obedience."

Democracy is a "foreign product" for the Chinese culture. For several thousand years, China has emphasized the culture of authority. Despite the impact of western democracy, Taiwan was not likely to be transformed into a fully democratic society in only 100 years. "Control" remains key to parenting in the Han culture of Taiwan. "Control" includes parental training of children, shaming, involvement with their children, exerting authority as well as encouraging autonomy, according to Ming-Yeh Wu, a sociologist in Taiwan specializing in family social research methods, adolescent issues and marriage and family relationships.[2] "Control" is easier with children. However, conflicts with adolescents can be significant.

Teenagers tend to be independent and to rely on their parents at the

---

[2] M-Y. Wu. Parenting Dilemma: Sociological Analysis of Parenting Teenagers in Taiwan, 2016.

same time. Taiwanese parents struggle with conflicting values of wanting their children to be independent and also to respect authority. In addition, the parents might have to cope with crises of middle age and might not simply be dealing with parent-child relationships or parenting. The parents of Taiwan wish to be "friends" with their adolescent children. However, they are still the parents. They control their children's pocket money, enforce curfews, and monitor their academic performance. At the same time, they expect their children to share their secrets and actively discuss their worries. These contradictions can create obstacles for the two parties.

In addition, Chinese society values interpersonal relations. Filial obedience and ethics are the core values to maintain family relations. "Filial obedience" in Chinese society and "child-based" concepts in the West reflect different values and beliefs. Western "child-based" concepts mean that children profit best from an emphasis on individualism. This Western concept supports the children's internal development. In Chinese society, the "child-based" concept means planning the children's lives, schools and after-school learning. The parents are busy picking up and dropping off their children and arranging their lives. They worry that their children will be inferior to other family members, to their friends' children or to classmates. The children's achievement is associated with the parents' "performance."

Planning is mostly based on the children's obedience to the parents. For instance, once the author was scheduling sessions of therapy for a child. After talking with the parents, the author realized that finding a time to see the child was challenging. On weekdays after school, the child continued with extra academics until seven or eight in the evening. On Saturday mornings, the child practiced Taekwando and in the evenings, there was a piano lesson. On Sundays, the child played soccer. The therapy could only be arranged on Saturday or Sunday afternoon.

In Chinese society, the children are mostly told this "control" is done for their own good. Children often view their parents as not skilled at or not interested in communicating with them or considering their needs.

In addition, traditional filial culture legitimates the meaning of

Chinese methods of parenting and of avoidance of conflicts between parents and children. These conflicts may be delayed. In the therapy room, it is common that grown-up children retrace their struggles and sacrifices with the parents' rearing in those earlier years. Hence, in the practice of child and adolescent psychotherapy in Taiwan, work with parents and establishing a working alliance with the parents is critical.

### Therapy in Taiwan

Psychotherapy developed very late in Taiwan. After the Second World War, with the assistance of the World Health Organization, psychotherapy-related training began to be introduced to Taiwan. The earliest phase of child and adolescent psychotherapy was based on "counseling" in junior high schools and elementary schools. Although there were counseling organizations, they did not require professional training or certification of their members. Counseling was part of the school curriculum.

The Psychologists' Act of 2001 in Taiwan required licensure of therapists for the first time. Before, there had been some child psychotherapy workers with professional training. The Psychologists' Act resulted in psychologists with professional licenses on school campuses and more child psychotherapists in the community and in medical institutions.

Child psychotherapy in Taiwan was initially based on play therapy. Afterwards, Kleinian therapy and Sandplay therapy were successively introduced to Taiwan.

The Taiwan Developing Group[3] of the International Association for Analytical Psychology (IAAP) was founded in 2010. Numerous professionals interested in the Jungian approach joined in. However, few of them practiced child psychotherapy and had only studied Sandplay therapy. In other words, the Jungian approach to child psychology in Taiwan was derived from Sandplay therapy. Jungian psychotherapy

---

[3] Developing Groups are associations of people in regions or countries in which there is no existing IAAP Group Member. The groups are composed of students of Analytical Psychology, working primarily as professional psychotherapists, physicians, and educators or in other relevant professions. A number of these may become Routers, pursuing training to become Individual Members of the IAAP.

for children and adolescents developed when the Taiwan Developing Group was founded, which invited Jungian child analysts to share their specialty in Taiwan.

The following two cases illustrate the special obstacles the larger Taiwanese culture and culture within families present in doing child psychotherapy.

## CASE 1: MIA

Mia (pseudonym) was referred for psychotherapy by the hospital. Mia's preschool teacher realized that Mia did not speak in school and suggested that the parents take Mia to the Child Psychiatry Division for an assessment. The psychiatrist diagnosed Mia with Selective Mutism and suggested that Mia should receive psychotherapy.

Before seeing Mia, I met with her parents and learned that Mia had a brother who was 18 months older than Mia. They told me that because of their work schedules, they had asked the father's aunt to take care of Mia and her brother. The children stayed with her during the week and returned to their parents' home on weekends and holidays. Due to developmental delay, her older brother received regular therapy in the hospital. Since Mia's brother was the eldest son, and in the family's thinking, boys are superior to girls, before and after Mia's birth, her mother had focused on her brother due to his developmental delay. After Mia was born and at the age when she should have started talking, the parents and her great-aunt treated her silence as being well-behaved and shy. Not until age four, with her teacher's long-term observation, did her teacher identify the abnormality and suggest that the parents should seek help. At that point, her parents started to worry about her.

Mia was brought by her father for the first visit. When I introduced myself and invited her to enter the sandplay room, she did not move and only stared at her father. I asked her if she wanted her father's company. She nodded. I told Mia that we could invite her father in at first and when she felt that she could stay with me alone, we could ask her father to wait outside. She nodded again and they followed me into the room.

When I had met her parents previously, they told me that Mia liked

Disney princesses. Therefore, I put the princesses in the sandplay room for Mia to see. First, I showed her around the sandplay room to make her feel comfortable. When she saw the line of dinosaurs, she said discreetly, "dinosaur." Since I had been informed of Mia's diagnosis of Selective Mutism, I had not expected that Mia would talk to me. At the second meeting, Mia was able to enter the room by herself, and her father waited outside. However, the father sat on a chair outside where Mia could see him if she opened the door.

In the following sessions with Mia and based on her parents' feedback, I obtained more information about the family. Mia's father came from a closely-knit family, and some of his siblings encountered financial difficulties. Mia's grandfather was the eldest son and thus assumed to be responsible for the family. He expected his eldest son, Mia's father, to take care of those in financial difficulties. When Mia's father mentioned this, he was embarrassed about the family situation.

As it turned out, Mia and her brother were looked after by the father's aunt, not primarily because of the parents' work situation, but because the family of the aunt needed her income as a babysitter. However, Mia's parents had noticed that Mia and her brother greatly resisted going to the aunt's house. They cried and screamed, and finally became hopelessly obedient. The parents did not take notice of the situation and thought that the children simply did not want to leave them. However, as my therapy progressed with Mia, I suspected that Mia and her brother were being mistreated at the father's aunt's house.

I recognized the father's difficulty. He was the eldest son in the family and since he showed better competence and financial status, he was expected to help other family members. According to Mia's grandfather, since the father's aunt was part of the family and since Mia and her brother needed a caregiver and the great-aunt had a flexible schedule, it was a win-win situation. I sympathized with Mia's father whose father extended his responsibility to his eldest son. Due to filial obedience and family ethics, Mia's father could not refuse his father. In addition, questioning the great-aunt's caregiving might affect his relationship with the relatives who would be embarrassed if Mia's father asked about how they took care of the children. Mia's father was uncertain if he could handle this complicated situation.

I told Mia's father that his father was in charge of the family and that Mia's father also had obligations towards his extended family. However, Mia and her brother should also be his concern. He was not only the son of his father, but also the father of Mia and her brother. After a while, since Mia's brother was going to attend elementary school, Mia's parents intended to transfer Mia to the kindergarten near her brother's school. In addition, the mother's working schedule changed, so that she could pick up the children and they no longer needed the care of the great-aunt.

Once Mia and her brother were certain they did not have to go to the great-aunt's house, they started telling their parents what had happened. Before, they had never talked about the situation and the parents thought they could not express their feelings because they were young. In a subsequent therapeutic hour, Mia began sobbing in the therapy room. She appeared as if she were in her own world and she did not respond to me. Finally, I asked her if she needed her father who was in the waiting room outside. She nodded. I told her that "We are going to see your Daddy and then we will come back to continue playing." She nodded again. I took Mia out. When she saw her father, she asked for a hug. Her father asked her gently, "What's wrong? Did you miss me? I was here." Mia gradually calmed down. She then said good-bye to her father and returned to the therapy room with me.

Mia had feelings of insecurity. Being placed in her great-aunt's house made her feel deprived of the relationship with her parents. I felt that when Mia cried in the therapy room and I took her to find her father, this was a very important experience for her: I would not deprive her of being close to her father--for her, I was a safe object, and she felt reconnected with her father. When Mia was able to connect with her father, she became more lively. Her connection with that animus was obvious: when Mia saw my ring on my hand, she asked me if this was given to me by my husband. I wondered if Mia wanted to make sure I had a protective animus figure in my life, like a husband, just as she had a protective figure in her father, so that the animus figure in my life would be there if we had children. When her session needed to be canceled for the holidays, she was angry with me, and many game scenes appeared in her sandtrays. I thought perhaps Mia thought, when I didn't see her, that I had abandoned her because I was with my own child.

During a later period of therapy, Mia enjoyed playing with two frogs. She called one of them "Lili" and wanted me to name the other. I called it "Sasa." Lili and Sasa often died and came back to life. In addition, Mia sometimes showed a family scene in the sand tray. However, the adults in the family often got up and left the house, while the children were sleeping.

I had now seen Mia for over one year. After the first month, she began talking to me in a low voice. By the end of six months, her selective mutism was greatly reduced.

Mia's therapy ended during the second year of therapy, when the family moved due to her father's job transfer. Mia was about 6 years old. The therapy had not reached a natural stopping point. I often wonder how Mia is doing.

CASE 2: RUBY

Ruby (pseudonym) was brought to therapy by her mother when she was in the 6th grade of elementary school. Her parents were having severe marital difficulties. Ruby's father had an affair and was violent to Ruby's mother. Due to these serious and ongoing marital problems, Ruby's mother considered divorcing Ruby's father. Ruby had a brother who was a few years older than Ruby. He knew more about what was happening between their parents than Ruby did. He sided with his mother which led to conflicts with his father. The divorce condition that Ruby's mother wanted was to have full custody of both children. However, because of the patriarchal culture, Ruby's paternal grandparents would not agree to this condition.

Ruby could feel that her father had "changed" and lost some interest in her, but since she did not know much about what had happened or about the attacks of her father and his parents on her mother, she identified with her father to some degree. In addition, Ruby transferred her feelings about the loss of her father's attention into anger against her mother.

On the one hand, Ruby's mother wanted to protect Ruby from being affected by the family conflicts and did not let her know much about these conflicts. On the other hand, she felt upset about what Ruby said to her. Based on her concerns about Ruby's adaptation problems and about Ruby's relationship with her, Ruby's mother started to bring Ruby to therapy through a friend's referral.

Ruby was quiet and silent in therapy room. I could feel that her body movements were very stiff when she first came in. She seemed nervous and did more than one sand tray in each session for the first few times. She appeared to be more comfortable after a while. Gradually she did only one sand tray in each session. The contents were rich, and occasionally she even made brisk body movements or hummed songs. Ruby did not mention what happened at school or in her life at home. Instead, I initiated questions to which she gave specific answers. As we continued to work, Ruby occasionally did two sand trays in a session. She did more sand trays when she was anxious.

Her craving for her father's attention could be seen from the first few sandtrays. She was born in the same month as her father, which was a special bond for Ruby. Ruby placed specific objects which represented "father" in the sand tray, such as briefcase and laptop, and put zodiac animals between her and her father. Although Ruby's mother tried her best to keep Ruby out of her parents' conflicts, Ruby still unconsciously sensed the loss of relationship with father, especially the attention of her father and his family towards her.

Her brother unexpectedly received more attention during this time, due to the traditional culture of patriarchy, and this attention appeared to Ruby to supersede her special bond with her father. Perhaps because Ruby could not bear this loss at first, she transformed the loss into anger against her mother: "My Dad doesn't love me because of my Mom, so it's not that I'm bad, it's not my problem, but my Mom's."

During the two years we worked together, Ruby also faced the transition from primary school to junior high school, while her brother was facing high school entrance exams and the increasing pressure of schoolwork. The Chinese family has always attached great importance to academic achievement, and Ruby's brother was better than Ruby in academic performance. His father and paternal grandparents put considerable pressure on Ruby's brother to achieve. They hoped that Ruby's brother could study in a top high school and through his choice of major in college prepare for a high-paying career. Ruby's mother did not agree with these values. She worked hard to maintain a space for choices for her children. Ruby's mother told Ruby and her brother that she would support the school and major they chose both financially and emotionally.

Ruby's parents did not get divorced, but after a period of time, reconciled. One of the conditions of the reconciliation was that in terms of living space arrangement, Ruby's father would live on a separate upper floor in the apartment, while the rest of the family lived downstairs. This arrangement allowed Ruby's brother to study with less interference from his father, and also made Ruby calmer. Ruby was less affected by her father because of her physical separation from him in their apartment, and she grew to understand her mother's situation better.

Although Ruby's brother had the love of family, he always loved and cared for Ruby. In the process of working with Ruby, I was very impressed with one sand tray: There was a bay on one side, and a boat on the sea on the other side. A boy sat in the boat and looked far into the distance. Ruby said that the boy was leaving, but he didn't know where to go. When I talked to Ruby's mother later in the session, I asked about the current situation at home. I learned that Ruby's brother was worried about which high school he would attend. I think Ruby may have felt the anxiety of her brother not knowing which high school to attend, but this may also have been Ruby's own anxiety: She began to stand with her brother, knowing what was going on in the family, but also losing her identification with her father: the development of her animus temporarily found no direction.

Ruby's mother was still worried that Ruby's father would attack her violently, therefore she privately arranged an emergency shelter and also let Ruby know about this place. Ruby gradually became closer to her mother. During summer vacation of the following year, Ruby's brother took part in a study tour to Europe, while Ruby and her mother traveled abroad. Ruby arranged and decided the travel schedule, while her mother was responsible only for booking hotels. Ruby was very happy and felt a sense of accomplishment. The trip meant a lot to Ruby and her mother. They completed the journey in a collaborative way. Under the protection provided by her mother, Ruby also had space for her own adventure.

My work with Ruby came to an end when Ruby was promoted to the final year of junior school and wanted to concentrate on academic preparation. In this course of more than two years, Ruby expressed herself through the sandplay, while my understanding of the changes in Ruby's external environment relied on regular feedback with Ruby's mother. Ruby's sand trays had many elements related to father. They showed her connection with her father, and also showed her beginning to sort out her relationship with her father and her loss of identification with her father. The relationship with her mother evolved from verbal attacks at the beginning, to which her mother stood up gently and firmly, to a positive connection between mother and daughter. The Chinese culture's preference for sons over daughters and emphasis on academic achievement were also challenges that Ruby faced and will continue to face.

For a long time, the themes of Ruby's sandplay were associated with home, rooms, sleeping quarters, and various activities. I remember once, Ruby squatted down in the corner of the storage cabinet and concentrated on one thing. I was very curious about what she was doing. I took a closer look and found that she was carefully arranging the food to be placed in the trolley. She then put this whole arrangement in the sand tray. I believe that in the treatment room, Ruby was organizing, creating, and preparing the nutrients she needed for her own inner development.

## Concluding Remarks

In Taiwan, the influence of history is deeply rooted in the collective conscious and unconscious. Taiwanese therapists, when engaged in the psychotherapy of children, must understand this context. Long-term anxiety about Taiwan's situation affects all aspects of life. For example, the emphasis on Taiwanese history relative to Chinese history relative to world history in primary and secondary education is constantly under debate and revision. Young people's and their parents' participation in politics and their political views are often quite different, and serious conflicts may occur in the family. These influences are actually hidden in the parents' views of nurturing, such as determining who decides, parent or child, what school their child will attend, what major they may choose and whether the child will stay at home for schooling or move away for their studies.

Taiwan's families struggle with issues of filial obedience, patriarchy and familism, issues we see with children in the therapy room. For example, Mia's father fulfilled his filial obedience at first, unable to play his role as father. With my help, he was able to understand his fatherly obligations to his children and to see those obligations as culturally appropriate. With Ruby, because her father's family favored sons, she initially sided with her father. Over time, and partly because of her brother's influence, she was able to take her place at her mother's side.

As Jungian therapists in Taiwan, we must remain constantly attuned to the uneasiness of parents as they try to make a secure place for their children in a country defined by its geopolitical vulnerability. In addition, parents are responding to the crosscurrents of traditional and more recent cultural influences. We must be ever attentive to the conscious and unconscious lives of the parents as we work to assist their children in therapy with the many struggles they face.

# REFERENCES

Chao, R.K. Beyond Parental Control and Authoritarian Parenting Style: Understanding Chinese Parenting through the Cultural Notion of Training. *Child Development*, 65, 1111-1119, 1994.

Chu, R-L. *Values and Cultural Attitude of the Taiwanese People in Religion and Culture: the 24th Conference of Taiwan Social Change Survey*, Taipei, Taiwan: Institute of Social Sciences of the Academia Sinica, October 30, 2015.

Li, G-L., Yan, Y-I., Xu, Y-J. *Illustrated Taiwanese Houses*. New Taipei City, Taiwan: Maple Bookstore Culture, 2017.

Lieber, E., Fung, H. & Leung, P.W-L. Chinese Child-Rearing Beliefs: Key Dimensions and Contributions to the Development of Culture Appropriate Assessment, *Asian Journal of Social Psychology*, 9, 140-147, 2006.

Wu, M-Y. *Parenting Dilemma: Sociological Analysis of Parenting Teenagers in Taiwan*. Taipei City, Taiwan: Wu-Nan Book, Inc., 2016.

# CHAPTER 6

# "The Womb of the Mother Spews Out the Führer"

## Batya Brosh Palmoni
### Rosh Pina, Israel

IN THIS CHAPTER, THE influence of being raised on a kibbutz will be discussed as it relates to an adolescent who was referred following a cutting incident at school and two years prior to the tragic loss of her father and an older brother. This chapter also explores the special challenges to be considered when living on a kibbutz is part of the family's narrative.

### Culture and the Family

Zohar (pseudonym) was born and raised on a kibbutz. The place where she grew up and developed is highly significant to understanding the psychological processes that shaped her world. She was born into a family with two older brothers, the younger of whom had severe developmental delays. Both her parents were Holocaust survivors, European Jews who came to the kibbutz after the war. One of the poems she wrote during therapy was about "the womb of her mother who spews out the Führer together with another six million children."

The story of the kibbutz in which she grew up is one of a group of young people who sought a place to realize a dream. From its beginning, the kibbutz was a combination of a commune that consumed collectively and a productive cooperative. The kibbutz demanded that its members undergo a personal revolution, centered on working the land and manual labor. Kibbutz members were committed to improving the personal traits of the individual, compared with the Diaspora Jews. Zohar's parents were devoted to the kibbutz and completely immersed in its values. However, their personal history—having no extended family at all, having a child with Down syndrome—made them an unconventional family in the kibbutz. Her father worked at different service jobs and her mother took care of children. Over the years Zohar's father descended into depression and was hospitalized. Zohar was born to an insignificant, closed, and distant family.

The kibbutz was founded by members of a generation of belief and ideology, a generation that undertook to perform extraordinary national tasks. There was a huge sense of mission. A profound testimony to this was seen later, in the first dream Zohar brought to the therapy. The pillars of the kibbutz structure were obedience to authority and belief in the wisdom of the leaders. Against this background, parents, and particularly mothers, were required to deny their feelings towards their children. The society undertook full responsibility for all the needs of the children.

The tension between the individual and the collective is a formative cultural complex in Israeli society and culture. The kibbutz is the place in which this tension is realized most dramatically. There is the tension of principles and ideology with personal desires, which are depicted, in contrast, as trivial and egotistical. Between the poles of strict ideals, at one end, and the emotional dynamic of collective life, many paradoxes arise. Individuation is extremely difficult and complex in the homogeneous space of the kibbutz. Using Neumann's terms, I would say that on kibbutz, the archetype of the Great Mother prevailed in the collective experience with a sense of a mystical common fate; and the Father archetype prevailed from the perspective of rigid rules and ideology, but without individuation.

One of the central complexes is related to otherness. Personal identity is always defined relative to some other, real or imagined. In a closed space, in which otherness is illegitimate by virtue of the array of social relationships, hidden and sometimes cruel variations of segregation and distancing are created. The otherness of Zohar's family was particularly striking and later, it was even more so. The process of adolescence for

Zohar—or any adolescent on kibbutz—involved a tremendous struggle against paralyzing conformism and the strong impact of the peer group. In this chapter, the focus will be on Zohar's process of developing a self-identity, which was intertwined, of course, with the emergence of and connection to the Self.

The collective upbringing in which Zohar was raised is a method of education by which children on the kibbutzim were educated from the 1920s until the late 1990s. In this form of collective education, the children from birth were raised in children's houses, not in their parents' homes. They saw their parents for just a few hours every afternoon. The collective education continued from infancy to adulthood. At the time, it was considered a natural result of the principle of equality, which was then customary in the kibbutzim, where the goals of the kibbutz and those of collective education were considered identical.

The kibbutz always appeared to be a fascinating human laboratory. From the start, it considered itself a community that focused on children. Kibbutz education in children's houses, with collective sleeping arrangements from the very beginning of life, emerged for several reasons, including physical and security considerations. Most of the kibbutzim were settled in difficult, remote locations because of their dedication to national goals. The decision to raise the children together stemmed from a need to protect them and provide them with the best possible conditions.

There were also two ideological trends that influenced the character of collective kibbutz education. First, the kibbutz championed elimination of inequality between the sexes. The thinking was that taking the children out of the home would free their mothers to pursue their own development. The kibbutz was also committed to the cultivation of the "new Israeli," a person well-prepared for collective life and work. The philosophers of collective education thought that by distancing the children from their parents, they would avoid irresolvable conflicts between the two, and particularly the Oedipus complex.

This second idea was, of course, dramatically influenced by psychoanalysis. The distancing of children from their parents was undoubtedly detrimental to the fundamental nature of primary relations. Understanding this is essential when considering the great difficulty of the children and parents in forming relationships and intimacy. Later, when René Spitz and John Bowlby published their research on attachment theory, the kibbutz also began emphasizing the importance of the parent–child relationship.[1]

Zohar was born in a period when the parents' home was considered slightly more significant, but the children's house and peer group still constituted the central emotional authority under which she and the other children were raised. The parents' house, known as "the room," was an additional center, albeit of secondary importance. The parents, nursery teacher, and peer group were the three focal points for the child's socialization. The process of Zohar's therapy and the productions of her unconscious can shed light on the process of this special adolescence.

## The Therapy

I chose to discuss Zohar's story and through it, to illuminate the important contribution of the analytical psychology approach to therapy with adolescents, with emphasis on the alliance created in therapy between the client, the therapist, and the unconscious. Analytical therapy enables clients to make their inner world present and their psychological life central. During therapy with adolescents on kibbutz, this process is complex, because it involves a forfeit of full partnership in the children's society. Thus, the therapy is aimed not at more successful processes of adjustment in the community, but at creating intimacy with the silenced and hidden life of emotions.

The psychological processes that the therapy activated were centroversion and automorphism, two central concepts in understanding the development of the personality according to Erich Neumann's approach.[2] Centroversion refers to a function of the psychological totality, which in the first half of life leads, among other things, to creating a center of consciousness. The center of consciousness, the "ego complex," is a sort of

---

[1] A. Lieblich, "Me'ah shana shel yaldut horut veshel mishpaha bekibbutz" ["A Century of Childhood, Parenting, and Family Life in The Kibbutz"].

[2] E. Neumann, *The Child*.

"branch" of the Self. Its aim is to serve the needs of the totality, in terms of the demands of both the inner world and the external environment. In this therapy, it was extremely important to address the real needs of the inner world, all those needs that it was impossible for Zohar to approach. Centroversion also refers to relationships between the ego and the Self and is related to construction of an ego–Self axis. When the primary relationships, in which the mother plays a central role in constructing the relationship of the child to her body, her Self, and the world, are damaged, the ego has to supply its needs from other sources, that is, without its central source of support, the Self. However, it not only has to fulfill these needs. It also has to care for itself, its fears, and its lack of confidence, all from its limited sources, because it has lost or not created a relationship with the Self, with the totality of the unconscious.

In a properly functioning primary relationship, the ego can rely on the mother and her love, as then an integral ego develops and the ego–Self axis remains stable. In Zohar's therapy, the distance from her mother, the collective education, and the difficult trauma she experienced caused her to disconnect from herself and did not enable the ego of the child, her personality, to develop its unique form—the automorphism.

Automorphism is a term that Neumann used to describe the unique specific orientation of every individual to fulfil his or her unique potential. It is associated, of course, with the development of psychological systems, the conscious and unconscious, and the relationship between them. Naturally, this process was also impossible, and Zohar was "found crushed and broken on the paving stones," as she described her situation later. Automorphism enables adolescents not only to experience themselves as the center, but also to experience the world as a place of belonging. This is not an experience of omnipotence, but a basic experience of proper human development. It is a process of unique self-creation. The solidarity of the ego and the Self is essential to this process. When this solidarity does not exist and the elements of security and unity disappear, the ego is left orphaned, emptied, and full of hunger, insecurity and helplessness. The development of a narcissistic personality is a typical compensation for this emptied ego. I would like to emphasize here that this was an adolescent who had been raised in collective education, where the relationship with the parents' home was limited and the peer group had a powerful influence, with tremendous pressure to conform.

An ego that is damaged in the primary relationships and detached from its inner sources, the Self, suppresses the maternal archetype and rejects it altogether. In this process, the relationship with the unconscious and Self are rejected, as well. In the process of development, in which a proper transition from the maternal, matriarchal layer to the patriarchal level is required, with centrality of the father archetype, the two layers are totally cut off from one another and the ego relies on and identifies with the father archetype. In the process of this detachment, a superego is developed that identifies with collective values and totally ignores the needs of the Self. This process is strongly intensified on kibbutz because it is a closed, ideological, and collective society.

The superego will always be a collective authority and its demands will always contradict the Self, the individual. In adjusting to these demands, a split occurs between the persona and the shadow. Loss of contact with the Self, which is the representation of the inner world, is simultaneously also a loss of contact with the external other. An attempt to compensate for this loss accelerates the development of a narcissistic personality.[3]

In this therapy, both the personal and the collective unconscious were central partners. Work with dreams was a central axis in the therapy. The possibility given Zohar during the therapy to get in touch with her inner Self and to observe her self-creation (primarily her dreams and later, the poems she wrote during the therapy and mental products), together enabled a change and transformation.

The symbols of her dreams served as fascinating developmental landmarks. Her temperament, her moodiness, her demands of herself and of me drove processes of growth and development.

Zohar was referred for therapy when she was 14 years old by her homeroom teacher and the school counselor. The reason for the referral

---

[3] E. Neumann, Narcissism, Normal Self-Formation and the Primary Relation to the Mother.

was an attempt to hurt herself by cutting her wrist on her right hand using a compass. She came with a background of a difficult, traumatic family story. Zohar herself told me her life story during the first therapy session. Two years before that, her father and her brother with Down Syndrome, who was 15 years old at the time, suffered a tragic death. In the two years that had passed since then, she suffered terribly from moodiness, introversion, and distancing from her age group, and from great difficulty in her relationships with her mother and those around her.

Zohar, who lived and had been raised on a kibbutz, was trying to survive this horrific disaster through a process that was essentially a minimization of human interaction. It was a process in which she gradually emptied herself of relationships and support, feeling threatened by any relationship that involved dependence, thus increasingly isolating herself. She relied on herself and did not feel a need for anyone else.

Zohar was physically attractive and had many talents. She danced and played music and was a good student. However, above all, she was extremely lonely. Therefore, I want to begin with the story of Narcissus, which first appeared in full in the third chapter of Ovid's *Metamorphoses*.[4] It is the story of a young man in love with himself.

The nymph, Echo, bothered Hera with her chattering and distracted her from noticing that her husband was being unfaithful. As punishment, Hera rendered Echo nearly mute: from then on, she could only repeat the last words that others said to her. Echo fell in love with Narcissus, the son of the nymph Liriope. Liriope had been raped by the river god and was carried away by the water while bathing. The product of the rape was a beautiful infant, whom all the nymphs cared for—Narcissus. From the beginning, there was fear for his fate, and when his mother went to Tiresias, the prophet, to ask about his future, he predicted that the child would live as long as he did not know himself. The boy grew up and became a handsome, cold, and aloof young man. Many fell in love with him, but he loved none of them. One day, Echo followed him when he was alone in the forest. From the bushes she watched him, amazed, so

---

[4] Ovid (Trans. S. Dykman) *Metamorphosot* [*Metamorphoseon*].

excited that she was speechless. Narcissus heard a noise and called out, "Is there anyone there?" Echo answered, "Anyone there?" And so their conversation continued:

> – Come!
> – Come!
> – What are you avoiding?
> – Avoiding.
> – Come out and we will meet.
> – We will meet.
> – I would sooner be dead than lie with you together.
> – Together.

Echo's sorrow was so great that she dried up and her body turned into a statue. Narcissus insulted many others who loved him. One of them placed a curse on him that he, too, would experience unrequited love. He wandered with inexplicable desire, seeking a purpose that he could not guess, until one day he sat down to rest next to a spring. The water was clear, and when he leaned down to drink, he fell in love with the face he saw there. He reached out to the beautiful young man until he realized he was looking at himself. Thus, he lay tortured, unable to stop looking at his reflection. Finally, he died of longing and weakness and was transformed into the flower that bears his name.

We will take one insight from this: one who loves a reflection without knowing it is his own does not actually know who he is.

The ability to reflect, and as a result, develop self-awareness, is compared with the narcissist, who is a shadow, a failure, one who does not recognize himself in his reflection, a narcissus sunken in the darkness of unawareness. Detached from his inner Self, he is a foreigner to himself and the world.[5]

Since Ovid's description in the first century CE and to this day, extensive literature has been written on the character of Narcissus and

---

[5] J. Kristeva (Trans. M. Ben-Naftali), *Sipurei Ahava* [*Histories d'amour*].

his female companion, Echo. They both served as a tremendous fountain and source of speculations about the human psyche.

The term "narcissism" first appeared in psychological theory as a term to describe pathological love of oneself and was usually accompanied by a pessimistic prognosis. To Freud, primary narcissism was self-love or ego-libidinal investment that prevents attachment. Secondary narcissism is the inability to distinguish between ego and object, producing a narcissistic personality that is closed to others.

It is most important in therapy with adolescents to consider the question of identity development. When we speak of adolescents and the process of adolescence, we must remember that the narcissistic stage is almost essential. Every adolescent has an intensive need to seek life in a world without limits, and self-love is necessary at this stage of identity-seeking. In this process, adolescents, of course, need reflection from the environment—sometimes desperately—in order to experience their sense of Self.

Analytical psychology treats the question of identity in terms of the existence or absence of a guiding force of the Self, which alone gives a person a sense of direction and a way, and as part of that, a sense of identity.

Analytical thinking made an important addition to understanding this disorder, because the damage is deep and primary, and only closeness to the unconscious, both personal and collective, creates a possibility of healing. The content that arises from the archetypical world will be used and serve the goal of transformation.

That same weak and damaged ego described earlier, which acts on the principle of survival alone, enables existence, but not the ability to cope symbolically with the paradoxes of human existence and interpersonal relationships. The paradoxes that are familiar to all of us—between separateness and unity, self and others, male and female, omnipotence and impotence, finality and eternality—are all possible when the ego builds the connection to the Self, and this connection enables containment of human complexity.

Prior to her referral to therapy, Zohar had tried to hurt herself more than once, thinking that death would be a refuge from her family and herself after the horrific tragedy of her father's and brother's deaths. Full of anger and rage, completely denied long before the terrible events in her family, she fled with all the power of her talents. When these too failed to calm her, she simply tried to eliminate herself by self-starvation. She was very talented—she played cello, danced, and since her birth had grown to satisfy the needs of her parents, particularly in mediation and adjustment to the kibbutz, as a normal, talented, intelligent girl who never knew who she really was.

Her family used her—not consciously, of course. Through her, they could feel a bit of belonging to the environment in which they lived, the kibbutz. It was a family in which the mother was weak and empty, and the father was loving but also violent and full of expectations of her. Zohar was not filled by herself, but rather by the expectations of her parents. When I asked her to tell me about herself, she chose to write the following:

> I am an oppressed sapphire
> That was thrown away from under the eyelashes of the purple-gray
>     clouds
> That was thrown away because there was never something that
>     someone could give me.
> I was a decoration on a chain of that old woman who threw me
>     away.
> Someone clenched her hand and drew tears from me that rolled
>     onto the paving stones.

Inflated grandiosity, on the one hand, and frequent feelings of terrible emptiness and being valueless, on the other hand. These feelings that Zohar experienced as central were the outcome of hurtful primary relationships. Thus, there was no chance at all that these aspects of the Self could develop and change, because she was doomed to be adult from her very infancy. She was in a state of loss and total breakdown of her personal identity. The Self was completely expropriated from her and swallowed up in the collective. She could not identify with either her father or her mother. Instead, as described in the poem, she was abandoned and exhausted on the paving stones.

From the beginning, the therapy enabled her to give voice to these difficult feelings that could never be heard —neither by her parents nor by the person caring for the children nor by the children her age. Thus, a grandiose mental mechanism was produced in Zohar that erased the gap between what she possessed and what she longed for. And, thus, this mechanism maintained the illusion that she was enough for herself.

In this period, the therapeutic relationship was essentially a transfer of tremendous psychological pain and my willingness to accompany Zohar in her great pain and bear it together with her. It was very important and central in the therapy because working in total unity with her enabled Zohar to develop. The connection and separateness are related to pain, to connecting with it and disconnecting from it. Zohar avoided close, intimate relations, which by definition threaten the basic omnipotent position because they lead to experiences of neediness and dependence, jealousy and rage. Naturally, her attitude to me was similar at the beginning of the therapy.

Indeed, she was an amazingly talented "sapphire," but with a tremendous need to be loved and admired by others, giving very little attention to others—and an infinite need for material objects from the outside. Her emotional life was almost empty, with very little empathy for anyone in the environment, along with restlessness, a constant search for other things to do, boredom. There was grandiosity as in the poem, megalomania, and nothingness. She held endless hate and anger that she did not recognize. It is important to remember that at home they didn't speak about the dead and didn't mention the reasons that led to the tragic events—the mother was fearful of any expression of feelings.

From the beginning of the therapy there were great difficulties in creating the therapeutic relationship. The first year of therapy was stormy and chaotic. She tested me endlessly, like difficult teenagers know to test their therapists. I knew that I had to pass her repeated tests. For example, when I would come into the waiting room to invite her into the therapy room, she would respond, "Wait a minute; I'm busy with other things," or she'd call me with dramatic requests to meet at impossible times, and when I couldn't accommodate, she'd send me letters about how it was so disappointing that at difficult moments I wasn't there for her. She expected me to be the ideal therapist for her—she had a tremendous need that I fulfill her unique needs that had never been met by her parents.

Zohar never received true recognition and approval from her parents, and the therapy had to correct this experience. It is important to remember that therapy should enable grandiosity and megalomania to occur and even be empathetic about them, so that these feelings can be processed and converted. It is as Neumann described the magic-phallic phase. In this developmental phase, the ego appears, but it is an overemphasized ego. It still lives in a united reality with the Great Mother but experiences itself and the world with a magical-omnipotent feeling. The ego at this stage has a magical outlook on the world. The reality is not objective. The ego grows stronger; it has a sense of power. This is a necessary and central process in creating a center of awareness of activation of the tendency to centroversion. The therapy with Zohar had to support these processes.

Many months after the relationship between us had stabilized, dreams began to appear. I want to say something general: work on dreams with adolescents is different than with adults. You must be especially cautious with interpretation. Interpretation is possible only when the therapist doesn't need to worry about another "presence" in the therapy. Until then, in my work with adolescents, I place much emphasis on the feeling function. For example: In the middle stage of the therapy, she dreamt:

> We saw bombs in the sky, we knew it wouldn't help us to flee or hide somewhere. We lay on the grass, knowing the bombs might fall. I hugged a small girl and calmed her and told her—close your eyes, don't be afraid, it'll be okay. And when we opened our eyes, it turned out it was a drill, there were no explosives in the bomb.

Here, for instance, a great opportunity arose to talk about the emotion that was developing in her, her ability to care for the little girl lying beside her, and her hugging her. How great this feeling was that was born in her and also seemed to have enabled neutralization of the destructive material in the bomb. Here I also hasten to say that the relational part of the Self emerged in this dream, but the path to the birth of the little girl was definitely long. The analysis of early experiences through dreams and therapeutic relations touches the depths and the region of the Self and frees it to build ties with the ego. There were endless dreams about bombs. The work on them was an opportunity to talk about the negative feelings, the anger, the jealousy, the despair, the disappointment that her family and her life story brought out in her.

The following is the first dream she brought to therapy:

> It was in my mother's house. My father was there, nevertheless. The pictures of my father and my brother were hung on the wall. I'm referring to the construction of a divider between the living room and the kitchen, which is composed of cubes with flowers drawn on them. On some of the cubes there were pictures of children. On the divider there were also two music stands. My niece arrived and the divider almost fell down. I tried to move my niece from there and then the picture of Dad fell and the glass shattered. When the picture fell on the floor, brown powder, like dry blood, fell from it. Mom stood next to me and a much larger picture was revealed to us, a picture drawn in charcoal of a man who died in the war. The man was lying in a field of thorns, dressed in old-fashioned clothing.

At my request, she drew the picture she had seen in a dream. In the picture she drew, a tree grew out of the head of the dead father.

She couldn't bear the death of her father. The trauma was painful, and she had difficulty touching on the intolerable truth. She built a completely different story that served her megalomanic needs, that her father died a hero's death at war. This was far from the truth, but Zohar gave his death a meaning that she could bear. A therapeutic dilemma arose here—how not to turn the story of the father's heroic death into a cover story that would weaken her coping strengths and serve false needs. Could the compensating description in the dream of the image of the father serve her processes of growth and development? At the moment, it was clear that the death of the father in a war, as the dream described, enabled survival, but it also allowed the emergence of an emotion of pain and loss. For the first time in the course of the therapy, she experienced deep pain and sadness. This dream enabled her to bring up memories of life with her father and with her developmentally challenged brother. As it is a first dream, the growing of the tree from the head of the dead father is a tremendously positive image, the emergence of the Self.

After this dream, an entire series of dreams of bombs appeared. The bombs fell from the sky or were held in her hand. It seemed that the entire world, the world on high and the world below, was full of danger of loss and destruction. It seemed that wherever she turned, everything was strewn with mines and bombs. Some of the bombs were round in shape and she experienced some of them as egg-shaped. In one of the dreams, she had to hold the bombs in her hand because any movement would annihilate her. These dreams had a tremendous effect on the therapy. We were able to experience the great danger awaiting her together, the destructive power of all the difficult emotions of rage and anger. We experienced life—especially the dangerous, difficult parts—together.

Zohar spent hours playing music alone in a shelter, dancing in a few rooms, running outside the kibbutz at night, going hours without sleep, and experiencing eating difficulties. Of course, as I said earlier, there was no place for commentary. Her talents also served her as a mechanism of self-destruction.

In this period, she wrote a poem:

A scarlet bomb falls,
Hitler plays the piano,
He gives a concert with the accompaniment of a choir, an opera of
    screams,
To the good corpses.
He sits in a living room
Painted pink
With one end destroyed

Like the womb of Mother. Hears only himself,
Himself times one million. And that's what bothers him in life and so
He kills in the quiet, to quiet his spirit and another million and
    another million.
Small swastikas fall on him from the sky
Until the piano breaks, the pink paint peels off and the womb of the
    Mother
Spews the Führer out.

We both felt clearly the terrible fear in which Zohar was living—the Holocaust of her parents, but also her personal holocaust, in which the womb of her mother held the Führer within her. The client underwent her holocaust for the second time but lived it in therapy for the first time. She experienced the painful recognition of an unbearable image of motherhood. Mother represented a true monster, and she did not have the strength yet to bravely stand up to this inner monster.

In the words she wrote, one can see how early the disturbance and how primary the damage was. In a womb like that of her Mother, it is impossible to grow. Not only is it impossible to grow from this womb, but such a negative connection with the mother creates a situation in which the inner world, too, not only the outer one, is experienced as full of hate and anger, a demanding and difficult jealousy.

Nevertheless, we were left with hope that was born of the possibility of being together with the very worst. And in the dream that I presented as an example, about the empty bomb, Zohar and I understood that the bomb existed, but was empty of explosives. Thus, it was possible to begin to deal with the negative emotions without fear of their destructive powers. The negative emotions towards her mother, her father, and her brother with Down Syndrome. Zohar remembered her father saying how talented and pretty she was, but underlying this sentence, which he repeated endlessly, was another, hidden sentence: if you do not provide for my needs, I am staying at a distance from you. And so, the experience of the need to remain only pretty and talented continued to grow.

Together with this, Zohar's negative emotions increased, but they were denied and repressed and fed the distance from her father, her mother, people, and life in general.

Many narcissistic clients talk about the extent to which their parents are proud of them on the one hand, and at the same time report a feeling of distance and uneasiness in the presence of their parents, which of course is unclear to them, but gives rise to intense rage and anger.

After a few months, two dreams appeared. In the first, Zohar dreamed that from within a box that belonged to her, a child developed. He developed well because Zohar and the family doctor took care of him.

The second dream:

> Two children with Down syndrome came to visit. One of them was very short, about one meter, like a dwarf. He was nice and friendly. The other, in comparison, was taller and he was very jealous of my being a friend of the first. I was taking care of the first child. And the whole time the first child tried to bother the second one. Mother told me in the dream that the first child was the son of another woman from the kibbutz who had died, and he was our guest.

Regarding the dream about the box, it was a new container, not the empty bombs of her first dreams. The box, in fact, was a vessel in which growth took place. The change began to be exciting—no longer bombs in the sky and in the womb, but human beings appeared. Zohar developed emotions and this was painful—the ability to suffer, the ability to feel pain, and especially, the ability to accept the Down syndrome part, her "damaged" brother, who at that time had already died. This led her to a reduction in her sense of grandiosity.

Strong feelings also emerged with these dreams around memories of life with her dead brother. During this process, she took the decision to give up playing music. Life began to be more human. And it took an adapted shape of its own; the choice not to play music was part of the process of automorphism that occurs with the formation of consciousness, with a center and creation of a connection to the unconscious. In this dream there was still the experience of the mother who couldn't accept the damaged parts and said that the child belonged to another mother, but Zohar herself began to develop her own shape. Positive human emotions filled this session. There was important psychological movement; there was space to move. For the first time, I talked with her about her damaged parts and the possibility of connecting to them.

Here we can see the beginning of the process of creating intimacy with the silenced and hidden life of emotions. When this process continued to develop, the psychological energy invested in narcissistic defenses was no longer directed to self-admiration and became available for discovery of the inner guide and connection with the Self.

For this transformation to occur, the personality had to overcome the identification with the inflated persona. This means that the difficult, hurt emotions and the trauma—which until now were in the shadows—could be felt and a new path opened for a different self-awareness. It's not that the narcissism completely disappeared, but now the consciousness could also bear the other side.

All the parts of the psyche that had been frozen, that were hidden by this complex, all the parts of the Self that could not be expressed until they now emerged in a process, where the therapist could share the tremendous emotional burden with the client. This dream in which the damaged part returned to life and was adopted by Zohar as a loved brother was a genuine and dramatic turning point in the therapy.

The therapy was accompanied by additional dreams about accepting the damaged parts or dreams in which she experienced the disappointing image of her mother. Although she was trying to follow her mother's eyes, as appeared in one of the dreams, she never was able to meet her glance. And the small child who grew up in the box in the dream—the brother with Down syndrome that she cared for—in other dreams became children that she raised and took care of, whom she took to the bathroom and protected. Her dreams enabled caring for, raising, and protecting her or caring together with her and not for a moment neglecting the healthy children that her psychologically good womb was growing within her, and always being in every place together with her.

## Conclusion

This therapy continued for a long time—more than four years. The relationship continued while she was in the army and afterwards. I conclude with a dream:

> We were poor and I lived with an old man and two boys. The three of us lived with him. We were eating breakfast. In the old man's room there was a box, like a casket. We asked him what was inside and he said there was wheat. During the day, a merchant came and bought the wheat, and in exchange did not pay him money, but instead provided what we needed each time, like winter underwear, blankets, sheets, etc. We didn't agree to accept this so easily, and nevertheless asked the old man to open the box. He opened it and we discovered that inside were winter blankets, bedding, and two pearl rings, and it was as though I was in the casket and outside of it, seeing everything.

The appearance of the old man was an image that contained practical treasures for her. Zohar, who identified so much with the inflated persona, had the benefit here of meeting the archetype of the wise old man, who has deep wisdom and treasures that are daily products, within her.

In the final chapter of his book, *The Child*, Neumann wrote about the Self in a slightly different way: in his view, the expressions of the Self undergo transformation in the course of life. And therefore, his understanding of the Self is different. According to him, the Self is not an archetype itself. The Self is reincarnated and takes shape through the archetypes in the process of development over the lifespan. Thus, it appears for the first time in the archetype of the Mother, later of the Father, then as a group Self, and only at the end as a personal archetype. However, the Self is not identical to any of these archetypes, but rather the archetype to which the Self is reincarnated is of tremendous importance at the same time as the ego. These changes in the embodiment of the Self are very important to psychological development. Every time the Self is reincarnated and freed from the archetypical incarnation that it first assumes, it takes its form, and then removes and destroys it.

This basic freedom of the Self and its lack of shape are extremely important to understanding the psyche and its development. In this last dream, the Self was reincarnated in the image of an old man, an expansion and correction of the image of Zohar's personal father.

The opening words of the dream—"we were poor"—were also so meaningful in the context of the change she had undergone—to make do with less, to live with what one has, and mainly, with who you are.

Nevertheless, the dream also opened the feminine side with which she was still so conflicted, in the image of the two pearl rings. The pearl is a gemstone, a symbol of the Self, and also a feminine principle of perfect femininity, which resided in the depths of her psyche. The pearl appears when the closed shell opens up. Zohar, who was so distant and detached from herself, an oppressed sapphire as she described herself, detached from her body and her feelings, from people around her, succeeded in letting go of her megalomania. In her dreams, she allowed herself to experience all the explosives and bombs inside her and was then able to raise a small child (in the dream) and even take care of her brother with Down syndrome, and the incomplete part within her. She dealt with the way her father had died.

The womb that spewed the Führer out became a box, a container that could grow children and take care of them, and when there were still bombs in the sky—lie on the grass and hug the little girl in her image with warmth and, finally, find a connection in herself with the man who was old and full of daily treasures, to look into the casket within herself and discover her femininity in it, as well.

Zohar matured and set out on her way. Later she met a young man. For the first time, she could see the other and make the transition to her femininity. For two years after her army service, we continued to keep in touch. When she was released from the army, she left the kibbutz, moved to the center of the country, worked and went back to dancing, evidently successfully. One weekend when she came to visit her mother, she was run over and killed by a driver who did not notice she was standing at the bus stop, waiting for a ride. I attended her funeral, crying deeply and knowing that she will always be part of what I am, she will always live inside of me, and her legacy will live on as others are touched by her story.

As in the poem by Dahlia Ravikovitch, in which "the man came back home to tell his sons of his death," so I, with your help, came back to tell her story and remember how important it is to speak about the dead, in order to illuminate and conserve all the pain and the beauty they left us. This is an eternal flower, the image of the Self, that remains next to the spring forever.

## REFERENCES

Kristeva, J. *Sipurei Ahava* [*Histories d'amour*], (M. Ben-Naftali, Trans.). Tel Aviv, Israel: Hakibbutz Hameuchad, 2006.

Lieblich, A. Me'ah shana shel yaldut horut veshel mishpaha bekibbutz [A Century of Childhood, Parenting, and Family Life in The Kibbutz], *Israel: Studies in Zionism and the State of Israel—History, Society, Culture* 17, 1-24, 2010.

Neumann, E. *The Child*, London, UK: Routledge, 1973.

Neumann, E. Narcissism, Normal Self-Formation and the Primary Relation to the Mother, *Spring Journal*, 42-67, 1966.

Ovid (Trans. S. Dykman) *Metamorphosot* [*Metamorphoseon*] Jerusalem, Israel: Bialik Institute, 1966.

Ravikovitch, D. 613 Mitzvot [613 Commandments] in *Kol Hashirim Ad Ko* [*All the Poems Till Now*]. Tel Aviv, Israel: Hakibbutz Hameuchad, 1995.

CHAPTER 7

# Jungian Child Analysis in Brazil

## *Lucia Azevedo*
Sao Paulo, Brazil

## Introduction

Jungian child therapy started to be practiced in Brazil in the 1970's, mainly in the major cities.

The Brazilian Society for Analytical Psychology (SBrPA), founded in 1978, was the first institution to offer training in analytical psychology. At that time, Jungian literature was already well known, and some of it was translated into Portuguese. However, at that time there was still very little published on Jungian developmental theory and practice of child and adolescent Jungian analysis, and still less published in Portuguese.

In Brazil, there was a certain tension between the Fordham-oriented and the Neumann-oriented professionals, similar to what happened around the world. It was always a challenge for the beginning analyst to find good useful literature and appropriate supervision of cases.

Nowadays, after more than forty years, the situation is changed much for the better. A big part of the significant Jungian literature is now translated into Portuguese. There are groups dedicated to studying and teaching child analysis in the SBrPA and the AJB ( Jungian Association of Brazil, founded in 1991). The Brazilian Society for Sandplay Therapy was founded in 2011, which also contributes to the training of child therapists. The early division between the two competing developmental theories is now, for the most part, in the past. There is much enthusiasm for integrating the "classical" Jungian theories with other areas of the study of human development, including psychoanalysis, infant observation, developmental psychology, attachment theory, and neuroscience.

Interest in Jungian theory and practice has been steadily growing these last decades, in addition to studies about its "translation" and applicability to Brazilian culture and realities. There are many professionals now dedicated to research and publishing.

However, psychological treatment and Jungian analysis are still very much a privilege of the upper classes, except for a few Jungian therapists working in the public health system or non-governmental organizations dedicated to working with less privileged groups.

Brazil is a vast country, and one of its main features is diversity, so it is impossible to speak of any "typical Brazilian family" or "typical Brazilian customs" without running the risk of reducing the richness of diversity and of stereotyping.

In order to convey a sense of Brazilian culture, this chapter gives some historical background on the formation of the country, its people, and culture, with special attention to the history of family structures and dynamics.

## The Culture: Historical Background

Brazil was colonized by the Portuguese, who arrived in 1500. At the time, there were a great number of different indigenous peoples, speaking hundreds of different languages. The main group living along the coast was the Tupi-Guarani. The social organization of this group presupposes that the men go away and marry elsewhere, while the women stay in the tribe and marry a man from outside the tribe. Marriage means a political alliance between the man and the tribe of the woman.

Since the Portuguese who first arrived here did not bring women with them, marriage with indigenous women was the norm. Through these marriages, some Portuguese were made very rich and very successful in the new land because they could count on the support of whole tribes who were now their relatives. The children of these first Brazilian marriages were raised by the mothers and spoke their language. Tupi-Guarani was the main language spoken in the whole south until the 18th century.

However, the indigenous women had to be baptized and take Christian names for the marriage to be recognized and accepted by the dominant Portuguese Catholic culture. Some tribes assimilated, but the Portuguese decimated other tribes that were not so easily assimilated. With time, indigenous culture was devalued more and more and the history of these first marriages and alliances almost erased from the collective consciousness.

Nevertheless, research with DNA conducted in recent years revealed that most Brazilians have indigenous and African genes from maternal ancestry. [1,2]

Starting in 1550, the Portuguese brought African slaves, mainly to the northeastern region. With the discovery of gold at the beginning of the 18th century, African slavery expanded into the whole colony. Slavery lasted until 1888.

In Brazil, differently from the United States of America and other countries, there was never a law prohibiting marriage between white and black people – Brazilian people are primarily mixed-race people. This is not to say that there is no racism; on the contrary, there is strong structural racism, mixed with class prejudice, which has started to be addressed by the collective consciousness and publicly fought against with more emphasis in these last decades.

Before then, the collective consciousness denied racism, believing that Brazil was a happy "democracy of races." It is true that at least in some places or some classes (mainly the poorer classes), mixed marriages have been common, but this does not mean that our shadow with racism is not a dark and challenging one.

This history also has consequences for other collective consciousness areas, such as a difficulty around superiority and inferiority issues. On the one hand, Brazilians sometimes identify with the European colonizer view and consider ourselves inferior: less intelligent, less productive, less organized, less serious – all these adjectives echoing the way Europeans viewed the indigenous and the African peoples. On the other hand,

---

[1] A.A.O. Xavier.
[2] H. Escobar.

sometimes we identify with some characteristics inherited from these cultures but which are admired: the sensuality, music, culinary, our *joie de vivre*, our talent in playing soccer, our adaptability to different circumstances.

Brazilian history also creates a difficulty with the matriarchal and patriarchal values in the collective consciousness. The culture has strong matriarchal traits derived from indigenous and African cultures and some aspects of Portuguese culture. However, the patriarchal law that arrived with colonization brought about an ambiguity in the collective consciousness. This law was identified as a value, but on the other hand, it was also identified with the oppressor, something "we have to find a way around." This ambiguity creates a shadow area, where the law is theoretically for everyone, but "not in my case." Our capacity to find a way around things is part of the folkloric self-image of the Brazilians – which can be valuable, of course. Still, finding a way around things can also be an enormous difficulty when it impedes justice and egalitarian rights.

These contradictions and cultural complexes are starting to come to the fore in recent decades. Much transformation is on the way, although with huge resistance.

In addition, there has been a considerable immigrant influx in Brazil, in the nineteenth and twentieth centuries, mainly to the southeast region: Italians, Spaniards, Japanese, Germans, Koreans, Chinese, Jews from Europe, Lebanon and Syria, and still others. Recently, there have been many refugees from South America, Cuba, and Africa. All of them come with their cultural baggage. Some adapt quickly to the new country, others with more difficulty, forming more closed communities. These immigrants add more complexity to the cultural and racial mix.

### The Family

One can consider the history of the Brazilian family as the history of arrangements negotiated between different cultures. The meeting of the two cultures, the Tupi and the Portuguese, in 1500, brought about a new kind of family.[3]

---

[3] L. Azevedo & M. Azevedo.

The structure and dynamics of the family have undergone many transformations during these five centuries. In the beginning, indigenous culture determined much of the family kinship rules.

For most indigenous peoples in Brazil, the child belonged to the father's group. The most common marriages were the man to either his sister's daughter or the daughter of his father's sister or his mother's brother. The husband usually lived in the wife's tribe, but sometimes the woman went to live with the man, generally when a chief gave his daughter in marriage to another chief to establish an alliance for war or commerce. This last case was the type of marriage that happened between an indigenous woman and a Portuguese husband.

It is important to note that marriage for indigenous people was not a sexual fidelity contract. It was an alliance with other goals, for example, economic: the couple and children were an economic unit that functioned in cooperation with other units of the tribe. Both the man and the woman could have lovers during the marriage. They could end the marriage and marry again; their children continued to be part of the father's group, lineage, or clan. As one of the preferred marriages was inter-generational, the uncle with the niece, it was not rare for the widower to marry again, with his niece and sometimes with the wife's sister.

When the Jesuits arrived to catechize the indigenous peoples, they were horrified with these kinds of families. They viewed those engaging in these marriages as lacking morals and lacking shame, especially the women, who arranged " lovers" for their husbands (in reality, they were arranging more economic and commercial alliances for their families). The Jesuits tried to legitimize these early inter-cultural marriages by baptizing the women and changing their names. These names are, until today, respected family names for Brazilian families whose roots go back to those early times.

The children from these marriages lived a double life: when they went to the country, they behaved as indigenous people. When they were in the towns, they acted like white people. Nevertheless, even among the official marriages and the higher classes, seen as representing the traditional patriarchal family, there were multiple arrangements and many differences between the official version and what happened in reality.

During the colonial and imperial periods (from 1500 until 1890), the extended family played an important role. Marriage between relatives remained widespread, mainly the uncle with a niece or between cousins, which were the preferred kinds of alliances among the Tupi-Guarani, even when this indigenous origin was not known.

In modern studies about the family behavior of Braziliait is evident that consanguineous relations as well as the solidarity built through vicinity and the *compadrio* (the custom at baptism of acquiring many godparents, who are considered part of the family, and who sometimes become the adults who take responsibility for the child) are central to family relations. In reality, these relations, first seen as incestuous, reveal the existence and collective acceptance of relationships that occur within the family, legal or not. Previously seen as an indication of moral dissolution, an analysis of these relationships indicates a family that can create connections of solidarity and affection. In this kind of family, the importance of women was much greater than in the patriarchal families. During this period, a large number of women were family chiefs.

With time, the upper classes became progressively more identified with the European patriarchal family pattern, and these arrangements became more prevalent among the population at large. This difference remains today, although the patriarchal conjugal family is now entirely dominant in the collective consciousness. However, strong connections within the community and within the extended family (grandparents, uncles and aunts, cousins, and others) and the *compadrio* still exist and are highly valued. These connections remain significant for nuclear families, especially among the working class and in rural areas.

In the big cities, the nuclear family is predominant, and since the last decades of the twentieth century, this nucleus has been left more and more alone to raise their children – father, mother, and children with less help and participation of the larger family or community. This change has put much strain on the parents.

Also, along with the rest of the western world, this kind of family is undergoing many changes. The number of children is diminishing, and the norm is two or three children. Marriage is not seen as indissoluble anymore, and separations, divorces, and second marriages are very common. Single-parent families (more commonly just mother and child, or less commonly just father and child) are also happening. In the last decades, there has also been a rise in the number of same-sex couples who have children.

There follows a description of what is most common among the middle-class urban families that are the predominant population of the private clinical practice.

Generally, both parents work and share the family's economic support, but most families still consider that support is the father's primary responsibility. Maternity leave is only four months long by law; the father has only one week. There is a solid movement to change this, but not with concrete results yet. Sometimes the infant stays at home, cared for by a nanny or the grandmother, although this last solution is becoming more infrequent. The baby may go to daycare center as soon as the mother goes back to work.

From two years on, it is expected that the child go to school, and for these families, private school is the choice. School lasts four to five hours, either in the morning or in the afternoon, which leaves half the day in which the child is at home – with a nanny or helper, or going to different kinds of activities, such as dance, music, arts, foreign language or sports. Depending on the family, the child ends up with a full calendar without much time for playing or resting.

Most middle-class families need domestic help to cope with all these demands. Until ten or twenty years ago, the rule was to employ a woman who slept in the house and helped with the domestic chores and raising the children, sometimes almost considered "part of the family." Frequently these women had to leave their own children with family members or with a neighbor, which could represent a non-verbalized source of stress inside the employer's family. Nowadays, the typical middle-class family has domestic help, but the relationship with these employees is considered more professional, and the women generally do not live with the family, going back to their own homes and families at night.

In recent years, more schools are opening, offering extended hours and other activities inside the premises, which is extremely helpful for these overwhelmed couples.

Also, in recent years, the work division between father and mother is more egalitarian, with the father sharing in the care of children and with domestic chores. However, we are still far from equal sharing of paid work, childcare and domestic work. Furthermore, it is becoming more common to have more flexible schedules at work, to better accommodate the demands of families with children. But in this respect, we are also still very far from true accommodations to the families' needs.

Among the working class and those in poverty, their children go to public schools, but depending on the family's economic need, they study only until adolescence or even earlier and leave school to start working to help the family. It is also very common to have the older children take care of the younger siblings or leave the children in the care of a neighbor or family member who does not work. These arrangements are more similar to the older traditions.

Brazilian parents are usually very affectionate towards their children; of course, the rules are stricter in some families than in others. In general, parents make an effort to supply their children with the best education and opportunities. The functioning of the family has changed from a more strict and patriarchal rule towards a more permissive one, and in some cases currently, we find the parents having difficulty establishing rules and limits for the children, at a loss as to how to educate without repression.

Also, in recent years, we have seen a rise in the number of immature and narcissistic parents who are self-absorbed or absorbed by their own careers and need of success, financial or professional, and this leaves less energy to dedicate to the children.

In addition, many parents are using more and more electronic devices to help calm down and distract the children, with adverse effects on their development.

Working in Sao Paulo with this population of middle-class families, I have seen families from many different backgrounds and cultures.

Apart from what we could call traditional Brazilian families, who have Portuguese background, many have one or more ancestors coming from Italy or Spain. Also common are Jewish families, whose grandparents or great-grandparents came to Brazil from Europe, many of them traumatized by war, or coming from Egypt, Lebanon, or Syria. I have worked with descendants of Japanese families, Portuguese, Danish, Swedish, German, and others. I have also worked with direct descendants from indigenous and black families – although these descendants are found more often in the working class.

Much as many families nowadays do not follow any religion, some degree of religiosity and spirituality remains pervasive: Catholic, Protestant of various denominations, Jewish, Kardecist spiritist, and the African-American syncretic religions, "Umbanda" and "Candomble."

So, to work in Sao Paulo is to train to have an open mind and sensitivity to many different cultural values. We need to understand and value the family history and the traumas and successes they have had in the past because these inform and illuminate the meaning of the child's troubles. We have to review our values and presuppositions constantly.

## The Therapy

This case was chosen because it beautifully illustrates the dynamics between patriarchal and matriarchal functioning modes when they are split and do not "marry." This problem is an integral part of the Brazilian shadow and has to be overcome to attain a needed transformation in the direction of mutuality, human rights, less economic inequality, preservation and caring for our fertile land, and healing.

Paul (pseudonym) was almost eleven when he came to therapy. His mother brought him because he was having great difficulty going to school. He had anxiety crises that prevented him from attending class and even had physical symptoms, including nausea, headache, and tachycardia.

Paul would leave his classroom and go to the school coordinator, who is responsible for attending to difficulties of teachers and pupils in each grade, both pedagogical and emotional. In this case, she was a very supportive woman. Sometimes he would stay in her room for the duration of the school day, and sometimes he was so anxious that his mother had to come to pick him up.

Until that time, Paul had never presented this kind of symptom. His mother described him as a normal child, affectionate, active, and independent. The only precedent his parents reported was bronchitis, which he had since he was a baby; it had improved very much when he was eight, after homeopathic treatment, but that year it had started over again. His mother also reported that he had had some nightmares in the weeks before the anxiety symptoms started.

In Brazil, an important change in the school happens when children are eleven. Through fifth grade, children usually have just one teacher who teaches them all subjects, except for physical education and sometimes arts or music. From sixth grade on, school starts to be more complex; there are more subjects and specialized teachers for different subjects. It is considered a significant change for the children, who feel they are beginning a new stage. They have to learn to relate to different teaching styles, and the relationship with the teacher gradually becomes more impersonal – the teacher through fifth grade usually is called "aunt," and the relationship with her is much more intimate and personal.

Paul was a little overweight, and he dragged his feet as if it were complicated to move around in the world. The overall impression was of a depressive mood; he felt awful about what was happening and had much hope about the therapy. In the first weeks of our work, Paul found it very difficult to say and even to perceive what he wanted to do – he always needed me to tell him what he should do. When I asked him about his preferences or desires, he generally answered with "whatever."

It was almost visible that he was being pulled downward or backward – as if he had chains around his feet, and something was impeding his movement in life.

Paul was the third child in the family – he had a brother and sister six and four years older. His family was Jewish, second and third generation descending from grandparents and great-grandparents who had fled the Soviet Union and Poland at the time of the Second World War. Although they lived comfortably, they were not very wealthy, and his father worked very hard to have economic success. I have observed that this task – to succeed economically in this new country – is often an unconscious or semi-conscious one passed on by the first immigrants to their descendants. This complex did not leave much energy for the father to dedicate to the children's education and to have intimacy with his family.

Father and Mother had agreed on the traditional division of responsibilities: the father was responsible for the economic support, and the mother was responsible for the emotional support. She had abdicated her professional development to stay at home and raise the children. Although dedicated and affectionate, at that time she was also beginning to feel frustrated about being just a housewife and wanted to explore new possibilities for herself.

Paul's dependency on her also frustrated her, although she was very receptive to his need for her presence and reassurance. She was worried about his development. Counseled by the school, it was she who initiated seeking professional help for Paul. The father deferred to his wife's decision but, for his part, considered that Paul was making a scene to impress his mother and teacher. He thought Paul's symptoms should not be taken seriously, or else he would be spoiled.

So, this family functioned in the patriarchal mode of consciousness, with a Split between the female domination within the family and the male domination in the outer world. Or, in archetypal terms, a split between the Sky Father (Zeus or Yahweh) and the Earth Mother.[4]

Paul was caught in the middle. Being the last child, he had stayed within the matriarchal domain up until that time. He probably had a good foundation for his development, but at this time, there was an ambivalence in the family towards his need to grow up and develop independence. In the consciousness, they all wanted it, but it was clear that there were resistances in the unconscious.

The fact that the father was emotionally unavailable complicated Paul's situation: when he needed his father's support, he met with judgment

---

[4] W. Colman, 522.

and criticism, which in turn caused him to be still more dependent on the mother.

I had the image that every time his ego tried to reach out for the archetypal realm of the father and the masculine, a Uranus-like father was constellated within the family, who pushed him back into the motherly realm, impeding his development. [5] His symptom of bronchitis already pointed to a constellation of being imprisoned inside matter, the *physis*.

One of the first dreams he told me in therapy depicted this psychic situation: "Some bandits had kidnapped other children and me. They wanted money as ransom to take us back to our families, but the fathers would not pay."

The first sandplay[6] he built showed a small town, with a man lying down on the corner with another waving beside him. He said: "He is ill, and this man is signaling for someone to come and help." So, the transference was a positive one with the therapy and the therapist: part of him was signaling for help, but I could feel in the transferential field that part of him was not confident that help could come.

We worked for some months with a few improvements: he was progressively more able to stay at school, his mother was a little less anxious about his progress, but his father still remained aloof and disconnected from what was happening.

One day, Paul built a sandplay (Figure 1).

He made a river, going from the bottom left corner to the upper right corner of the sand tray, and put a small boat with a man inside almost in the right corner; he poured sand on both corners and said: "I will tell you a story: they were sailing, but then a barrier fell here (upper-right corner) and here (lower-left corner), and then they could not go on. They sailed back and forth, and they still thought they were going somewhere, but they were not." Then he put some men with shovels near the boat and completed: "They were trying to clear the way." Finally, he looked at me

---

[5] M. Stein.
[6] Note all sand trays have been reconstructed due to poor quality of the original images.

**Figure 1. River, island and manned boat**
(Photoraph: L. Azevedo, 1998/2021)

and said: "At least I am trying, you see," in a way that left no doubt about his knowledge of his situation.

This image showed me that the therapy was also in this boat that was going nowhere. I decided I had to redouble my efforts with his parents, trying to help them understand his need for the father and create more opportunities for Paul and his father to be together. I was trying to help in a very concrete way the *coniunctio* of father and mother, so it could also happen inside Paul's psyche.

I believe that including the work with parents is a significant feature of child analysis, contributing to helping work through the parents' complexes and liberating the child's development.[7,8]

Paul could not regress to an infantile state, dependent on Mother; the negative aspect of the archetype was threatening to devour him, rendering him paralyzed and suffocated. However, neither could he progress in the

---

[7] L. Azevedo, et al.
[8] S. Zemmelman.

direction of the masculine world because he was being pushed back as incapable of meeting Father's demands.

## Initiation by Fire and Water

After some time working "back and forth" with these two opposing forces, Paul started to experiment with fire in his sessions. Up until that time, he had been afraid of fire and knives, perhaps still listening to echoes of mother's admonishments. It started when he found a toy car that changed color when put in hot water; he was delighted when he found out he could light the fire in the small stove by himself, heat the water and put the car inside it. He gradually became less afraid of matches and the fire. Then Paul found some old crayons and started to melt them and mix the melted colors with an old knife.

He became bolder than before. One day a drop of melted wax fell on his hand, and he was frightened, but soon he realized that he was not seriously burnt and continued to work. When he left the consultation room, he went to his mother and proudly showed her the burn on his hand.

I understood it was a big step for him in the direction of autonomy and the mobilization of his courage to face the "dangerous" world outside. I also understood that he was alchemically working with the *solve et coagula* alchemical maxim: dissolving his archaic infantile fears and solidifying new ways of dealing with the world.

One day we found out that a great number of small caterpillars had invaded my little garden and were threatening the survival of one of my favorite shrubs. When he saw my dismay, he promptly offered to get rid of the caterpillars for me. I immediately felt like I was a damsel in distress, and he was bravely coming to save me from danger! The hero archetype had been constellated. What a change in the transferential field!

So, of course, I agreed, and we passed many hours killing the caterpillars – but he did not simply kill them; he hunted them and burned them using his recently conquered mastery over the fire, or else he cut them in pieces, using his knife. (I had to make an effort not to feel sorry for the caterpillars.)

One day he had melted wax on the knife and put it again in the fire;

the wax caught fire and created a flame on the knife: he was fascinated – he had created a flaming blade! The phallic symbol was clear, and I immediately remembered the angel with a fiery sword expulsing Adam and Eve from paradise. How wonderful that he had been able to incorporate this symbol of archetypal masculine power in his ego! It was one numinous moment in the process.

At the same time, Paul interspersed the fiery sessions with "watery" sessions – he would go to the sand tray and pour water on the sand, gradually becoming bolder and creating bigger and bigger floods. I could concretely observe the dissolving of the blockages he had built for the river where the boat was going nowhere. For some time, he created such a big flood that it was also impossible for any boat to sail there!

He also started to create big waves, which would escape the sandbox container and would "accidentally" fall on the walls or the floor. But it was not an accident – I could see the pleasure he felt when his waves escaped the boundaries. He would look at me a little frightened at first, but when I provided a bigger container, covering the floor with a resistant piece of plastic, he could exceed the boundary of the tray without fearing destroying me in the transference as a container for his impulses, either creative or destructive.

It soon became a game: he would pretend it was by chance he was splashing the floor; I would pretend to be annoyed or angry about it. We both knew it was a pretending game, and I understood it as his need to rehearse how to use his masculine power to escape the constrictions of the maternal container, to prove himself potent to be able to defy Mother in her suffocating and devouring aspect.

For some time, this game went on; then, he started to build islands in the sandbox, which at first were destroyed by waves. One day he decided to make a huge island that would withstand the force of the waves. He was delighted when he did it, and I was too – it was another numinous moment in this process: the solidification of his ego, now with the necessary masculine strength to withstand the force of the emotions and the difficulties of life.

During this time, Paul was able to attend school without having anxiety attacks anymore. However, he had transformed from a "good boy and a good student" into an "enfant terrible": he joined with other boys at school, and together they provoked the teachers and other children, creating disturbances during the class – once more he had to leave the classroom, but this time as a punishment from the teachers.

It took all the trust we had built between the family and me to prevent the parents from being completely frustrated with his transformation. This development also made it necessary to change the family dynamic; in the beginning, they just wanted Paul to continue being a good son and a good student without the anxiety. However, his path provoked everybody to have to come to terms with his aggressive and destructive impulses, with the "bad boy" side of himself: all that was left in the shadow, Paul's personal shadow, and the family shadow.

I continued working with the parents, and sometimes Paul wanted me to help convince them of something he wanted – for example, he had decided to pierce his ear with an earring, and his father was adamant against it. I knew I could not play the role of his advocate before the parents because he had to trust his own power to do what he wanted. The risk here would be that I would substitute the personal mother in the role of his protector from the terrible father, thereby repeating the pattern all over again and once more castrating him. There is always the risk of being captured by the family complexes when we work in child therapy, and it demands being very attentive and careful to prevent the therapist from becoming prey to the pull of pathological family dynamics.

One day, after the summer holidays, Paul came to therapy very angry with me and with life in general: I had interrupted the sessions to enjoy myself, and he could not go to a holiday camp he very much wanted to go to, because his father had told him it was too expensive. He tried to provoke me, caught some toy spiders and insects, and threw them at me; I interpreted his behavior as his frustration about the holidays, and then he went to the sand tray.

He put many soldiers in the tray, all attacking two dinosaurs, which "wanted to invade the world." He said: "They are powerful. They step on the people." Then he removed the dinosaurs, put a witch in their place,

**Figure 2. Witch, soldiers and fleeing horses**
(Photograph: L. Azevedo, 1999/2021)

and put a fence around the tray, with some horses running away over the upper right corner (Figure 2).

He explained: "She invaded a farm; everybody is afraid of her, the soldiers and the animals. She wants to devour the world, eat everybody. She wants to rule over the world." Then he put a table, a mortar and a Coca-Cola bottle in front of the witch.

He thought a little and said: "I could swallow the witch, and then I would be the ruler of the world." He appeared to ponder this possibility but changed his mind: "No, I would become the witch's friend and would help her kill everybody. Then, when she was sleeping, I would take my knife and cut off her head…. And then I would make a lot of test-tube babies and people the world again. It would take millions of years…. He laughed and added: "But I had to become friends with her, otherwise how could I kill her during the night?"

It was a "mythical moment" in the therapy. Paul finally confronted the devouring witch! His story resembles a myth of creation. Interestingly, his solution is a trickster story and not simply a heroic one. He does not trust only his physical force, but he counts on his intelligence and resourcefulness. He has to trick the witch into believing he is a friend and sleep with her – the reference to incest is clear – but his goal is to kill her when she is vulnerable, although at first he considered identifying with her to rule the world! I was glad that he did not succumb to this omnipotent temptation.

This kind of solution is parallel to the mythologem of being swallowed by the monster and then killing it from the inside. Paul's adventures with the creation and mastery of fire also reminded me of the hero who lights a fire inside the monster's belly. Moreover, he could only accomplish the witch's killing because now he owned his fiery knife!

Nevertheless, his solution is only a partial one because in killing the witch, he perceives he also destroys the feminine principle – it is very interesting that he intuitively tries to solve this problem, making "test-tube babies" to repopulate the world. This is still an omnipotent solution; it is part of the archetypal mythology of patriarchy and male domination, where the masculine is identified with the procreative principle, which was the realm of the Great Mother.[9] I understood it was a necessary step in his individuation process when his ego had to be freed from the Negative Mother pull.

After this session, Paul continued to play with fire, water, and sand. He continued to show defiant behavior in the school and at home, but he was progressively able to engage in argumentation to back up his wishes and requests. He wanted a dog, and although his mother did not want to, he could convince his father, and they could engage in a project together – to find and care for the dog. It was a significant transformation inside this family.

Paul made a picture of a cave by the sea, in the sand tray (Figure 3).

He put many people around it, on the beach, on boats sailing at sea, and a man about to enter the cave to explore it. Above the cave, two children were playing, a boy and a girl. I was happy to see the feminine principle represented here, as an anima figure who could play with him "above" the maternal cave, which was now a place to explore and no longer the negative imprisoning womb. This development calmed my fear of a unilateral consciousness, the way Hillman puts it: "the ego development

---

[9] W. Colman, 537.

**Figure 3. Beach, boats and cave by the sea**
(Photograph: L. Azevedo, 1999/2021)

**Figure 4. Volcano with village**
(Photograph: L. Azevedo, 1999/2021)

which has the hero as the model will have as part of this model the shadow of the hero – alienation from the feminine and compulsive masculinity – prefiguring the bitter and sterile senex as a result of the heroic way."[10]

After a while, Paul decided to join fire, water, sand, and melted wax from the crayons into a sandplay.

He built a large volcano in the middle of the tray, with the melted wax representing lava flowing towards the sea (Figure 4). He told me the volcano was erupting, and many people came to watch. Apparently, the eruption was not considered dangerous, and it was more a spectacle. There were some small houses nearby, and also some boats at sea. He lit a fire inside the volcano and asked me to take a photo of this extraordinary moment.

It was another numinous experience in his process. The lighting of the fire inside the mountain was awe-inspiring, and we both were silently observing it happen.

I think this was a Self-picture; it was like a grand finale of his process. He asked to leave the image intact until his next session, which I did. I knew he needed the permanence of the tangible symbol to appropriate its numen and strength.

After that, Paul gradually became less interested in the sandplay and other activities in the therapy room; he wanted to play ball and found me wanting in his need for a match. After a few months, we decided it was time for him to end therapy, and he entered a soccer training class held at the same time as the therapy used to be – what I considered symbolically very pertinent. The treatment lasted two years.

His parents also were happy with his development. After some time had passed since the end of therapy, I met his mother by chance, and she told me she had started a new job and was very happy.

After seven years had gone by, Paul came to see me again. He was twenty years old, and he was going to Europe with a group of other young people. It represented a sort of initiation rite for them. He was afraid of not being able to travel so far away from his family and country

---

[10] J. Hillman, 132.

and wanted to reassure himself with my opinion. We reviewed his sand-plays and his process together; he did not remember much of what had happened, but he could see that he had inside himself something solid to support himself – something he could trust. I was also pleased to know he was doing well and had a girlfriend. Such is the power of sandplay – the pictures are a concrete image of the inner psychic process and can be referred to when needed.

## Concluding Remarks

The archetypal problem of the *coniunctio* of Father and Mother has been worked through in many different ways throughout human history, as we see in the vast number of myths and folkloric stories dealing with this theme.

In Brazil, since the first marriage of a Portuguese man with an indigenous woman, the culture has struggled with this problematic *coniunctio*. The meeting of the western patriarchal culture and the indigenous and African cultures was one of dominance, repression, and abuse. Among other consequences, it created difficulty in integrating matriarchal and patriarchal values and modes of consciousness, causing an ambiguity in the collective consciousness.

In the 21$^{st}$ century, we are seeing the expansion of the consciousness of these shadow complexes and are starting to seek reparatory actions. Still, we have a long way to go. Each individual also has to come to terms with these polarities; there will be different ways depending on one's culture, personal history, and stage of development. In the analysis process, we can follow how the individuation path of each client deals with this theme, as the case related above showed.

It is exciting to follow the partial resolutions that the Self finds during the therapy of children and adolescents. Many symbols that are individually worked through resonate with our time's cultural dilemmas and contradictions. For example, many children now go through a stage in therapy when they try to find a way for humans and animals in the wild to get together without destroying each other. This can also be seen as an attempt to find a way of marrying the Father-culture with Mother-nature.

When these archetypes are not split, different parts of the whole can better communicate and enter in dialogue, either in the individual or the collective.

# REFERENCES

Azevedo, L & Azevedo, M. A Familia Brasileira – *Anais do II Congresso Latino Americano de Psicologia Junguiana* [The Brazilian Family – *Proceedings of II Latin American Congress of Jungian Psychology*]. Rio de Janeiro, Brazil: 2000.

Azevedo, L et al. O Lugar da Familia na Terapia na Terapia Infantil Junguiana. [The Place of the Family in Jungian Child Therapy". *Desafios da Prática: o paciente e o continente; Anais do III Congresso Latino-Americano de Psicologia Junguiana.* [*Proceedings of III Latin American Congress of Jungian Psychology*] Salvador, 2003.

Colman, W. Tyrannical Omnipotence in the Archetypal Father. *Journal of Analytical Psychology*, *45,* 521-539, 2000.

Escobar, H. DNA preserva história de populações escravizadas no genoma dos brasileiros. *Jornal da Universidade de São Paulo,* November 4, 2020. https://jornal.usbr/ciencias/ciencias-biologicas/dna-preserva-historia-de-indigenas-e-escravos-no-genoma-dos-brasileiros/

Hillman, J. A Grande Mãe, seu filho, seu Herói e o Puer. *Pais e Mães [Fathers and Mothers].* São Paulo, Brazil: Ed Simbolo, 1979.

Stein, M. "O Pai Devorador." *Pais e Mães.* [*Devouring Father. Father and Mothers*]. São Paulo, Brazil, Ed Simbolo, 1979.

Xavier, A.A.O. DNA Dos Brasileiros Carrega Marcas da Colonização. *Com Ciência: Revista Eletrônica de Jornalismo Científico. (SBPC),* November 9, 2020. https://www.comciencia.br/dna-dos-brasileiros-carrega-marcas-da-colonizacao/

Zemmelman, S. Working with Parents in Child Analysis and Psychotherapy: An Integrated Approach. In Punnett, A. (Ed.) *Jungian Child Analysis.* Sheridan, WY: Fisher King Press, 2018.

CHAPTER 8

# On the Russian Culture and Family

*Elena Bortuleva and Viktoria Andreeva*
**Moscow, Russia**

THIS CHAPTER DISCUSSES HOW the child's development is affected by the family's belonging to the "Russian" life and style—its history, geography, and culture--and mainly, by speaking the Russian language. All these and, perhaps, other factors contribute to creating a cultural skin,[1] a transitional space where one's inborn expectations and symbolized personal experiences are mediated to be taken into one's identity. We put "Russian" in quotes because almost the majority of those who live in the Russian Federation and who had lived in the former USSR, now citizens of states independent from Russia, have spoken Russian but not all of them considered themselves Russians. This chapter attempts to illustrate, through clinical vignettes, how the cultural complex can easily merge with personal complexes and cultural traumas and by this merging, make a powerful defense against the child's need and wish to individuate.

We know that children who have developed symptoms and/or show difficulties in adapting socially try by these behaviors to communicate their psychic pain to their parents and the therapist when help is sought. In their suffering, very often two messages are heard--a cry for liberation from some invisible, yet, powerful oppressor and an inner deeper, archetypal or

---

[1] B. Feldman. The Cultural Skin in China. In *Research in Analytical Psychology: 1ˢᵗ Edition* (C. Roesler, Ed.).

natural, urge for individuation, i.e., for becoming who you really are, for learning how to live according to one's own needs and feelings and yet, be a part of a broader community. These needs and feelings in many children and adolescents often remain undiscovered without psychotherapy. Far too many families are unable to provide an emotional container for them to grow through opening to the new. Very often, the child's feelings are difficult to reach, for them even to be mirrored and differentiated from the family's unconscious where transgenerational trauma is usually an intrinsic part of every therapeutic case.

According to Cavalli,[2] this trauma affects generations differently. The first-generation experiences trauma, the second one dissociates from it and acts as if it is not there, while the third generation embodies the trauma. This pattern appears in the three generations of Russians, starting from the outbreak of World War I which became a socialist revolution, to near the end of the twentieth century, who grew up under the ideas of Communism which started to 'soften' in the 1970s, which were considered the years of the Soviet Renaissance. This difference in manifestations, we often find, makes children who come to see psychotherapists look like aliens to their own parents and especially grandparents. Intergenerational trauma turns the generation gap into an abyss, sometimes unnavigable. Every complex, as Jung discovered, is capable of acting as a separate personality until it is found out, lived to the full, and integrated. Similarly, the trauma complex with its intolerable pain, rage and shame, making the child feel extremely vulnerable, will reveal itself repeatedly until it is 'fully understood'[3] - the rupture/s discovered, the pain tolerated, named, and contained.

In all the generations, although in varying degrees of intensity, the issue of communicating the child's feelings to their parents is feared or dreaded and either denied or avoided. As noted earlier, very few families have been able to provide a sensitive emotional container to their children. The infant, child and adolescent very often has been given a rather

---

[2] A. Cavalli. Transgenerational Transmission of Indigestible Facts. In *Trauma to Memory, Symbolization and Narrative*.

[3] A. Cavalli. Moscow Seminar. September 13, 2014.

mechanical, "factual" container allowing one's physical survival, which later allows the child to become a container for the parent, as opposed to becoming individuated.

The Russian cultural complex, with "Russian" here being a term of which we will say more later, is inseparable from the collective trauma of Russian history, both glorious and terrifying, and, specifically, from the so-called "Russia's 20th century," the century which started with a series of revolutions and the perpetration of a totalitarian regime targeting all individual diversity, and ended with the political and economic collapse of the Soviet Union and the difficult birth and growth of the nation-state called the Russian Federation, which has created its own trauma and stress.

## Between the Anvil of Geography and the Hammer of History

You are the large,
You are the plenty,
You are the powerful,
You are the powerless,
Sweet Mother Russia. [4]

I want to ask if I have a right to...
Yes, you have.
So, can I...?
No, you can't [5]

Russia is one of the largest countries in the world. Her earth is rich in prehistoric remains and she is exceptionally diverse in geography, climate, ethnic composition and languages and, hence, in local cultures. It seems easier to shoot for Mars than to define what it means to be culturally

---

[4] N. Nekrasov. Who is Happy and Free in Russia?
[5] Anecdote of 1934, the year preceding the onset of the state-run policy called the Bolshoi Terror, quoted in E. Fainalova's podcast, From Lenin to Putin, on Radio Svoboda, 2020.

Russian, bearing in mind the diversity and controversies stemming from that diversity.

At various times, various minds tried to define what it means to be Russian. It has been necessary to understand who we are--what is the Russian character or Russian "mysterious soul" like? We can look at the cultural complex, by putting to the forefront the vastness of a territory rich in animals, minerals and crops (hospitable, generous to prodigal; kind and humble to naïve, yet also arrogant and challenging). We can look at climate, the long, harsh winters of the ancient European Plain on which the bulk of Russia sits (unsmiling, stubborn and generally difficult people, yet, enduring and resourceful). We can examine the centuries-old "learned helplessness" based on the practice of submission of numerous individual wills to the peevish will of some powerful and/or ruthless, superior, a Big Man, due to the long tradition of serfdom, beneficial for the hierarchical military state perpetuated in the Romanov empire to be transformed later to the full-scale "party discipline" in the Soviet empire (obedient to passive, non-negotiable, phobic, rigid, suspicious and unpredictable under threat, real or fantasized, however, sacrificial to "not counting the costs"). Finally, we can think about Russian sensitivity to culture (open-minded, curious, talented, inventive, insightful, creative to provocative, etc.), and in all sectors of society there is a colossal tolerance for violence.

One of the lessons learned by the Russian people throughout their history is that it can always be worse than it is now. The survival capacity Russians have developed in the course of time is, perhaps not surprisingly, interlaced with humor and irony. The modern Russian writer Denis Dragunsky in a radio talk with his fellow writer Dmitry Bykov defines Russia as the country spreading along the Southern coast of the Arctic Ocean. His rather humorous definition illustrates this paradox of the polarization pertinent to the Russian people, helping some to survive by approaching the center (both writers live in Moscow), and others by moving into the Russian vastness (Anton Chekhov's steppe), keeping a safe distance from the strong ones. "Beware of masters, they // Will cause you trouble any day.// Of all the woes may God deliver us from both// From their love and their wrath."[6]

In the 20th century Joseph Brodsky formulated this principle in his poem:

I am sending you, Postumus, these books.
What's in the capital? Lying softly? Isn't it tough for sleep?
How is Caesar? What's he doing? All intrigue?
All intrigue, probably, yes, gluttony...
I am sitting in my garden, a lamp is on.
No girlfriend, no servants, no acquaintances.
Instead of the weak and strong
Of this world – only the insistent hum of insects...
Perhaps, my Postumus, a chicken isn't really a bird to be admired,
The chicken brains will get you grief and woe.
Yet, if it falls to be born in the Empire,
It is better to live in a remote province by the sea.
Away from Caesar and from the blizzard.
No need to fawn and hurry or be a coward...[7]

The vastness of Russia's territory is truly impressive. If you take the fastest plane and fly from Vladivostok to Moscow it will take you four hours to reach the Ural Mountains and five hours more to land at Sheremetyevo International Airport (nicknamed Sharik, the ball). Observing first the vastness of eastern Russia from the plane, the greenness of her rather monotonous taiga, randomly relieved by spots of blue water including Lake Baikal, the world's largest fresh water supply and then, once over the Urals, which form the natural border between Europe and Asia, you see a sudden change of landscapes, giving you a special pleasure in staying awake while passing through nine time zones.

---

[6] A. Griboyedov. *Wow from Wit,* Act I, Scene 2.

[7] J. Brodsky, Letters to a Roman Friend (after Martial).

Not every Russian tsar or emperor witnessed the country they owned from boundary to boundary with their own eyes. Yet, their power dictated that Mother Russia could live without her people but never without a tsar.

Russian history since the death of Peter the Great in 1725[8] shows the ebbs and flows of two opposing tendencies--on the one hand, the formation of the nation-state based on the Russian language and culture and Orthodox Christianity, using a western model; on the other hand, the perpetration of unlimited power concentrated in the hands of one Big Man in the Byzantine tradition. The ethnicity or gender of this Big Man never really mattered. In the veins of Russian tsars, tzarinas and monarchs, as well as their gentry and serfs, flowed Scandinavian, Polish, Tatar, German, Italian, French, English, Georgian and other blood. The power of this Big Man was almost boundless, at times not limited by either people or the fear of God. The Big Man tendency overshadowed a much more tender, although persistent, trend towards shaping a society of individually responsible and equal citizens.

Even today, the dominance of a Big Man (be s/he a tsar/ina, a Communist party leade—a "Communist tsar"—or a president) over Russia's geography and history remains mercilessly exploited. This dominance is promulgated , both literally and metaphorically, as a supreme blessing. The geographical (also geological) uniqueness of Russia, a sort of chosen-ness, in conjunction with its glorious and tragic historical path can overshadow and denigrate one's individual search for truth, making it unimportant and meaningless. Just like Tolkien's ring of omnipotence, the uniqueness of Mother Russia has played a double role. Viewed initially as something attractive, yet plain, accessible and supple, it can turn into a seductive and enticing primeval deity capable of blinding those who attempt to identify with its power.

---

[8] Y. Lotman, Russian Literature of the Post-Petrine Era and the Christian Tradition. In Yu, M. *Lotman and the Tartu-Moscow Semiotic School*, 368.

## On the Language and Apprehension of Beauty

The newcomers shifted from foot to foot.

"We have come to see you, Professor," said one whose shock of...hair rose at least six inches above his head, "on a matter of business..."

"You, my good sirs, are most unwise to be going around without galoshes in weather like this," Philip Philipovich interrupted him reprovingly.

"In the first place, you will catch cold and, in the second, you have left dirty footprints all over my carpets, and all my carpets are Persian.

The one with a shock of hair was struck dumb and all four of them gazed at Philip Philipovich in amazement....

"In the first place, we're not gentlemen," pronounced the most youthful of the four...

"In the first place," Philip Philipovich interrupted him, "are you a man or a woman?"

The four of them again fell silent and their mouths fell open...

"What difference does that make, comrade?" he inquired proudly. "I am a woman," admitted the youth ... and blushed...

"Don't sir me," said the blonde, taking off his hat.

"We came to you," the one with the shock of hair began again.

"First and foremost, who are we?"...

"We, the house committee," Shvonder began with hatred, "have come to you after a general meeting of the inhabitants of our block at which the question of reallocation of living space stood..."

"Who stood on who?" Philip Philipovich raised his voice. "Be so good as to express yourself more clearly"

"The question of the reallocation of living space stood on the agenda."[9]

Russia's 20th century was a special period in its entire history. It started with a set of revolutions which eventually overthrew the three-centuries' old Romanov empire down to its foundation (as they sang in the Hymn of the Internationale) and established the Soviet state, which would collapse in the 1990s, *de jure* but not *de facto*.

[9] M. Bulgakov. *The Heart of a Dog*, 15.

In the excerpt above, Mikhail Bulgakov marks the onset of the process of creating 'the country of the empty sky.'[10] This two-dimensional structure started, as Bulgakov shows it, with the attack on bourgeois beauty via the riddance of gender differences and by the legitimation of bad manners and hatred towards home comfort and one's personal, non-collective style of thinking and living. In this excerpt we can feel a future clash of cultures – the sophisticated against the crude. And in this clash at times the frames will become blurred or eliminated. The newly established culture will be finalized in the image of Stalin clad in his eternal overcoat and speaking his harsh rhetoric, both messages of double-bind nature.

Bulgakov shows the beginning of a large-scale change of established Russian social norms. Soon they will be gone forever, wiped away by the rage and pain of millions and millions of 'the insulted and humiliated'.[11] This major change impacted the Russian language, which would become lexically simplified and overloaded with Communist formulas. Softness and mutual respect in person-to-person communication, tenderness and erotic feelings gradually were supplanted by group 'deep satisfaction' or even mass public approval with regard to a top party speaker's words and speeches, never mind how disrespectful or false they were. The outside and inside worlds were purposefully simplified, flattened and made colorless. That process was reflected by the language which turned more and more formal, dry and rigid. Bulkagov's group of people clad in dark leather, wearing dirty boots, enter the private apartment of Professor Philip Philipovich Preobrazhensky (whose name refers to transformation) with a sense of entitlement and the right to bring damage to one's individual life. This small passage highlights the transition from Russian to Soviet at various levels of one's being. This transition will soon put an end to old traditions of beauty.

"Russian" in English stands both for ethnicity and for national affiliation regardless of ethnicity. "American" in English is equally inclusive. However, the Russian language has two words, one for ethnicity and one for nationality. The word (plural) for ethnicity is *Russkiye*. The word for

---

[10] E. Radzinsky. Why Ancharov? In G. Schekina, *Collection of Essays, Vol. 6,* 67.

[11] F. Dostoyevsky. *Insulted and Humiliated.*

nationality is *Rossiyane*. According to the Merriam-Webster Dictionary in the United States, the word *Russki* (since 1840) can be used as a disparaging nickname, justly or not pointing to the national shadow, often one's projection in the search for an outer enemy.

The end of the Soviet Union, a "red" empire, according to the Nobel Laureate in literature (2015) Svetlana Alexiyevich, triggered the convergence of *Russkiye* and *Rossiyane*. The Soviet Union this "red" empire, the utopia embodied through a huge social experiment, was inhabited by a supposedly new breed of people with minimal diversities, even in gender, thanks to an overall policy of erasing individuality. Kindergarten and school specialists were to be ideologically approved for that purpose. Boris Yeltsin, Russia's first president, made efforts to put *Rossiyane* into wider use, probably to distance it from the various bombastic and derogatory connotations of *Ruskii*, also in the sense of *Sovietskii*, so that this convergence could contribute to the nation's formation based on the principles of democracy and individual responsibility. Yet, according to Alexiyevich,[12] in her Nobel Prize speech, the "red" empire ended but the "red" man persisted. Three generations of the "red" men lived "among executors and victims,"[13] belonging to either or both of "these" two Russias," according to Anna Akhmatova.[14] Education for children implied readiness to die for their Soviet "Motherland."

This "red" man embodies our cultural shadow with its generationally unprocessed pain, rage, horror and shame, muted and hidden in inter-ethnic and inter-denominational marriages, many of which resulted not from people's individual choices, but from almost 80 years of social disruption due to revolutions, a violent Civil War, an unprecedented resettlement policy, and state-based terror practices "against a variety of groups (from peasants to bureaucrats, and from intelligentsia to jazz fans)." This "path" also includes two devastating world wars, numerous military conflicts in which the Soviet Union took part, as well as Olympic Games which were akin to "special operations."

The major social experiment is over but the pain and incomprehension

---

[12] S. Alexiyevich, Nobel Prize speech, 2015.
[13] S. Alexiyevich, Nobel Prize speech, 2015.
[14] L. Chukovskaya, Notes on *Anna Akhmatova, Vol. 2*, 1952-1962, 41.

of "What has this been?" and "Why has this happened to us?" persist. The past overshadows the present and future. We are still locked in and by our unprocessed feelings and unasked questions that make us feel different and, thus, unique. According to philosopher and sociologist Grigory Yudin,[15] Russian society feels isolated without and "atomized" within.

However, the Russian language and culture continue to exist. Currently, outside the former Soviet Union, Russian-speaking people are associated with ethnic Russians. This perception makes some expatriates feel united and happy while others angrily protest, for they desire to distance themselves from the common cultural trauma. From 1922 until 1991, we, as we believed and were told, belonged to a new human breed called "the Soviet people" with some 350 million individuals populating the former fifteen Soviet Republics of the USSR. Speaking Russian was then a norm, natural or imposed. Since the former "Soviets" transcended political borders, the former communal life, much-loved by some and equally hated by others turned the Russian language and Russian culture into a unifying base for a large number of people around the world. People who are neither *Russkie* nor *Rossiyane*, like the writer Svetlana Alexiyevich, a Belarus citizen, use Russian as their *lingua franca*. It allows many people to stay updated by listening to Russian speakers on radio, TV, YouTube or other internet platforms, as well as mentally nourished by Russian classical and modern books, often audiobooks now, magnificent Soviet animation, and beloved Soviet films and modern Russian serials through which they recognize themselves as coming from the Communist Atlantis.[16] We former Soviets who speak Russian, whether ethnic Russians or not, share the same past with its traumas and the same language to help us speak for the voiceless and those silenced by the cultural trauma.

The Russian language, as we know it today, is directly associated with Alexander Pushkin, who raised its colloquial base to bridge the gap between the vernacular and the speech of the nobility, making it friendly

---

[15] G. Yudin. Who Are We – Individualists or Collectivists? December 6, 2018.

[16] E. Radzinsky. Why Ancharov? In G. Schekina, *Collection of Essays, Vol. 6,* 67.

to multiple Latin-based neologisms. The Russian language as part of the culture has been a great collector and knowledge-gatherer. From the seventeenth century until 1917, the court and the gentry of the Russian empire spoke several European languages. In the nineteenth century, the French language and French lifestyle became a role model. Ordinary people tried to follow the trend. For almost two centuries, Russia was possessed by Gallomania. As children copy their love objects, Russian high society copied the French way.

Denis Fonvizin, an eighteenth-century descendant of the Varangian (Viking) Prince Rurik and of Polish and German aristocrats, a graduate of the Moscow Imperial University and student at the medical faculty in Montpellier, a secretary to Count Panin, and a confidant of the German Princess known as Catherine the Great, wrote a Russian literary comedy highly prized by Griboyedov and Pushkin. In Fonvizin's satiric play the main character says: "My body was born in Russia, this is true; yet, my spirit belongs to the French Crown."[17] A century later, the "peasant" Count Lev Tolstoy in his epic *War and Peace* writes: "... Prince Vasiliy Kuragin, a man of high rank and importance ... spoke refined French in which our **grandfathers** [the bold is ours] not only spoke but thought...".[18]

Starting in the middle of the nineteenth century, Russia began to show it did not need role models anymore, for she entered the late adolescent period which developmental psychologists mark as the consolidation of one's identity. This period is associated with the flowering of Russian culture and sciences which branded Russia as the country of Tolstoy-Dostoyevsky-Chekhov, of Russian ballet, of Mendeleev's periodic table, of Ivan Pavlov's reflex theory and of Stanislavsky's contributions to the theatre. Russia was becoming an integral part of the European community. This flowering continued into the twentieth century, leading to the historic flight of Yuri Gagarin.

The Red October Socialist Revolution (official name) of 1917 ended the 300-year-old Romanov empire. The art and culture of that empire

---

[17] D. Fonvizin. *Brigadier-General*.
[18] L. Tolstoy. *War and Peace*, Chapter 1.

were threatened as well. For this was the revolution of the 'humiliated and insulted,'[19] the most oppressed, Russia's darkest underground. The pain from the unhealed wounds inflicted by the millennium-old serfdom, formally abolished in 1861, was replaced by the totalitarian bondage established by the Communist Party and its "Communist tsar," a Georgian, Joseph Dzugashvili, known as Stalin (made of steel), and turned into a weapon of revenge. Every cultural achievement became the object of persecution and destruction.

The list of Russian-speaking men and women of culture, the true gold of the nation, expelled by the regime or eradicated from within is so long and impressively sorrowful that it defies comprehension. Modern writers and scholars continue to search for language to describe what happened to Mother Russia (then the Soviet Union) during the "Bolshoi Terror" of 1936-38 and beyond and have not succeeded so far.[20]

The Russian language with its literature and poetry became both target and weapon. This civil war of the radical vision of Communism versus the diverse and individual led to "the complete withdrawal of [the old] reality."[21] The Russian language was meant to become suitable for Soviet neologisms, for serving a new esthetic and aesthetics--"to the ground, and then..."(see quote below). Its message was expressed in the words of the new country's anthem (1918-1944). The new-old song, taken from the French *L'Internationale*, written by Eugène Pottier in 1871, was cut to three verses with a repeated chorus, slightly modified in words and much in meaning in the Russian translation. It became an atheistic state's prayer. *"We are going to destroy the whole world of violence// to the ground//, and then// we are going to build our world, a new world.// Those who were nothing//are going to become everything...."*[22] Three generations of Soviet people "went through" this Soviet education, targeted at creating

---

[19] F. Dostoyevsky. *Humiliated and Insulted.*

[20] M. Chudakova. Interview with journalist Leonid Velekhov on Radio Svoboda, 2015.

[21] V. Martynov. *The Motley Twigs of Jacob: On the End of the Time of Russian Literature*, 140.

[22] *The Internationale.*

steadfast tin soldiers for the sake of building some new world, "went through" being a typical Soviet-period neologism.

After Stalin's death in 1953, amnesty was issued and streams of political prisoners (called the Bolshoi Rehabilitance, a fusing of Renaissance and Rehabilitation) from inaccessible areas of permafrost and the eternal Russian wasteland filed into city courtyards. Russian style and language received new infusions in the form of camp habits, dress code, neologisms and sparkling anecdotes from "people-pebbles" with a specific inner world,[23] the rolled stones, rolled by the harsh waves of Soviet gulags, the Soviet rock-n-roll venues. Applying the myth of the baby Zeus, which Thomas Singer uses to describe the cultural complex underpinning the western world, Mother Russia is going through the stage of development that precedes her pregnancy with the infant Zeus. We are still dealing with a devouring and insatiable father in anticipation of the emergence of the idea and conviction that mindfulness can limit madness (baby Zeus surrounded by Kourethes).

## The cultural complex of parent-child relationships in the post-Soviet space

The main questions that arise during parental consulting are probably the same anywhere in the world: the quality of the child's interactions with their parents; personal boundaries; the forming of the child's personal space; respect for the child's personality; awareness of the child's needs and efforts to understand them.

When studying the psyche, Jungian analysis rests upon the cultural complex, which goes deeper than the personal story. According to Jung, the psyche is layered, and the *individual* lies on top of a much thicker layer, that of the *collective*. Henderson[24] introduced the concept of the *cultural complex* as the layer situated between the personal and the collective. Morgan suggests that the cultural complex "underpins the archetypical forms or predispositions, and it is as the archetypical moves through the

---

[23] A. Solzhenitsyn. *One Day in the Life of Ivan Denisovich.*
[24] J. Henderson *Cultural Attitudes in Psychological Perspective.*

social, cultural and personal filters of the unconscious that it is filled out into an image or an idea that emerges into consciousness." [25] According to Singer,

> Cultural complexes structure emotional experience... cultural complexes tend to be repetitive, autonomous, resist consciousness, and collect experience that confirms their historical point of view.[26]

In this chapter, we will look at the way this aspect of our parent-child collective unconscious developed over the last century. The history of twentieth-century Russia is terrifying. All its milestone events are tragic; when we study it, we see obliterated generations and immense traumas that have persisted for years and decades. Luigi Zoja writes:

> ... collective trauma that befalls upon both adults and children and is remembered for generations can become the nidus around which a cultural complex forms and it might be better if analysts became more aware of and concerned with cultural complexes ... the psyche reacts to trauma by regressing to an archetypical pattern. [27]

The culture of childhood and parenting underwent such radical change over the past hundred years that debris from all this destruction is still flying around, getting into our eyes and hearts like the splinters of the Snow Queen's troll-mirror, killing love and destroying the soul.

In the first part of the twentieth century, the Communist revolution led to civil war, sowing discord first and foremost within families. The country was engulfed by the revolutionary complex, the core of which is the demise and murder of parent figures. We murdered the tsar, we murdered teachers and intellectuals – all the figures that opposed the

---

[25] H. Morgan, Exploring Racism, *Journal of Analytical Psychology*, 47, 4, 579.

[26] T. Singer, The Cultural Complex and Archetypal Defenses of the Collective Spirit, *The San Francisco Jung Institute Library Journal*, 20, 10.

[27] L. Zoja, *The Cultural Complex: Contemporary Jungian Perspectives on Psyche and Society*, 137.

revolution. The obliteration of religious traditions, the tearing down of churches and executions of clergy and royalty amounted to the demolition of authority and with it, of positive Self-images. The result was a constellation of the negative Shadow image of the Self. For decades, the country remained buried under this shadow. A new ideology was created with the aim of disrupting traditions and moral standards; the goal was to turn individuals into obedient creatures who would serve the country and fight its wars. Over decades, the ideological machine deepened the chasm between generations.

We all had one father: Stalin, the Father of Nations or the Master of the country. The souls of children internalized this shadow figure. Family and paternity traditions were demolished; the personal had to be sacrificed to the collective. The history of Russia and other Soviet states is an example of ways in which a dictatorial regime replaces an absent father.

The regime created a new mythology that also applied to child-parent interaction. One of the central figures of this mythology was a small boy called Pavlik Morozov. His father was against the official collectivization policy, and the boy betrayed him to the authorities, who shot him, in line with revolutionary practices. Essentially, Pavlik was made a hero for getting his father killed. For many years, Pavlik Morozov remained an official role model for children. In other words, the new regime was purposefully destroying family values. Other children were supposed to take the cue from Pavlik. In the 1970s and 1980s when the authors were young schoolchildren, this hero was still held up as a role model.

Children were forcefully separated from their parents. Soon after birth, many parents had to send their babies to nurseries where they stayed overnight for five days a week. This means that a mother would go back to work a month or two after giving birth, and the families only spent time with their children during weekends. Nurseries were built near factories so the mothers could come and breastfeed their babies, and that was it. It goes without saying that a true bond cannot be developed under such conditions. This practice lasted for quite a while in Russia, resulting in several generations of children who grew up apart from their families.

In 1920s, the Red Terror started, with repressions against millions of innocent people lasting for almost three decades. The regime would proclaim someone "an enemy of the people" on ideological grounds and either send them to a concentration camp or execute them. There were special camps for the victims' wives and children. Children who weren't incarcerated were forced to disown their parents, otherwise they were denied access to education or work. "Your father or mother is an enemy and unless you admit it and disown them publicly, you are an enemy and subject to execution too."

The Second World War left millions of orphans. Children lost their parents and homes. The most famous Soviet-Russian semiologist, linguist and anthropologist Vyacheslav V. Ivanov writes:

> In a sense, the twentieth century is so dreadful because it showed us how far a part of humanity can go to destroy the other part. My insights into Russian history and the fates of Russian intelligentsia in the twentieth century are about the obliterated generations.[28]

Then came decades behind the iron curtain of the USSR with its collectivization and destruction of everything individual.

In terms of Jung's theory of development of the soul, we were offered anti-individuation: collective, guided consciousness. There was no respect for a child's personality. Freedom of self-expression was impossible in a totalitarian state. Children had to comply with the standard of the Procrustean bed, and the parenting function was thus externally defined. Society intervened into marriage and child raising. We graduated school in the Soviet era, and we remember how we used to wear uniforms, take part in marches, and thank the government and Lenin for our happy childhood during every public celebration. It would have been funny if it hadn't been so sad because the cultural complex comes to life inside an individual, potentially causing serious disorders.

It's Russia's job to help other nations to understand its unique and horrifying

---

[28] V. Ivanov, *The Lord Sleeps Between the Lines*, 160.

historical experience... It is moving in this direction very slowly. Unfortunately, it goes in circles, falling into traps set quite a while ago. [29]

In many ways, our development can be defined as a tough obstacle race; we move forward in spite of the circumstances, not due to them. Understanding our historical experience is currently an important goal.

In the book, *The Cultural Complex: Contemporary Jungian Perspectives on Psyche and Society,* Thomas Singer writes:

> First, there is a continuum in the content and structure of complexes that ranges from the personal to the cultural to the archetypical. At the same time, some complexes have become such a part of a group's identity over time and repetitive experience that the cultural level of the complex becomes dominant or paramount, even in the psyche of an individual. Individuals are frequently swallowed whole by the group complex that has come to define their ethnic, religious, racial, gender or other primary sense of identity.[30]

In contemporary Russia, the perception of the parental function is polarized just as the society has been, following the collapse of the Soviet Union. In Russia's vast countryside outside of big cities, families nostalgically try to raise "sons of the nation" who will defend them against enemies, from both without and within. To this day, the dominant model of raising and educating children relies on forceful separation and strict upbringing that prepares them for a hard life.

During parental consultations, we often ask parents why they picture such a future and what kind of hard life they expect their children to have. Most often, this starts them talking of their past. We can see them reproducing their entrapment in the trauma that many of us share: the trauma of survival and existence instead of life. One cannot survive if one remains a mama's boy or girl.

---

[29] V. Ivanov, *The Lord Sleeps Between the Lines*, 160.

[30] T. Singer. The Cultural Complex and Archetypal Defenses of the Collective Spirit, *The San Francisco Jung Institute Library Journal, 20,* 22.

## Therapy with Children and Work with Parents

Here's an example from the case treated by one of the authors involving a five-year-old girl, Masha (all children's names are pseudonyms). Her parents brought her to see the therapist because she had a whole range of disturbing symptoms: diurnal and nocturnal enuresis, facial tics, frequent rashes, numerous fears, disturbed sleep and inability to stay anywhere without her mother.

Diagnosis revealed an abyss between the little girl and her mother. The girl's imagery was cold and distant, reflecting a shortage of strength and resources. During consultations, I encouraged the mother to join me in the effort to understand their relationship, but soon hit a wall: "I need time for myself, don't you see? I have three children and I spend plenty of time with them."

I suggested the mother should see a therapist and try to improve her understanding of her child's tragedy; the girl's symptoms were her way of screaming in pain.

**MOTHER:** *Why should I see a therapist?*

**THERAPIST:** *You could try understanding your daughter, what frightens her so much and why, what kind of anxiety doesn't let her sleep, what makes her scream and wake everyone during the night.*

**MOTHER:** *Why should it have something to do with me? Maybe she's just a sickly child. Maybe she has weak blood vessels and that's why she always wets her bed. Opinions vary. She gets a lot of my attention compared to my other children.*

The mother said that her other children spend less time with her and don't mind it in the least. They don't have problems with bedwetting or rashes. She is annoyed that her daughter wants her attention all the time. The mother's internal abandoned child is used to getting hurt and doesn't complain. It was treated harshly and has stopped screaming, and now it meets this little girl asking for her mother as she used to. How can the mother handle this?

This mother makes me think of the recommendations given by doctors in our hospitals and teachers at our nurseries. "When a child cries and finds separation difficult, the mother needs to leave quickly, so the child doesn't grow weak. It's better to leave unnoticed, to distract or deceive the child." They say that a young child will soon forget. Nursery teachers sometimes criticize a parent who stays to console a crying child. A child can be left alone at a hospital; parents are often not allowed. Many of these memories are relived at the therapist's office.

Masha's mother had a typical Soviet childhood, she was regularly sent to stay with her grandmother for extended periods. At her grand-mother's, she often got ill, expressing her grief physically. Her mother was strict and busy; the child was not allowed to cry. At age two, she became gravely ill when her parents sent her to her grandmother's for six months. When she was six, her mother gave birth to another daughter, and she had to stay at her grandmother's again for over a month. She had otitis and problems with digestion. Parents like this often say: *"What's the big deal, I was beaten as a child, yet I grew up and turned out fine."*

Tischler[31] points out in work with parents of psychologically very ill children, the parents' unconscious perception of their own parents as weak or cruel can easily be enacted with the child. The child is perceived as a reminder of the child within the parent, suffering again the same fate as the parent did in childhood. Or the child, as a reminder of the grandparent who is unconsciously feared and hated, is not treated as himself, but is mistaken for another.

I tried to show this mother the ties between her past and her present. I wanted her to see that the broken link between mother and child gets reproduced, and that she could at least try to repair it.

Fraiberg, Adelson and Shapiro[32] introduced the metaphor "ghosts in the nursery" to describe the ways in which parents, by relational experiences of helplessness and fear, transmit child maltreatment from

---

[31] S. Tischler. Being with a Psychotic Child: A Psycho-Analytical Approach to the Problems of Parents of Psychotic Children. *International Journal of Psycho-Analysis, 60.*

[32] S. Fraiberg, E. Adelson, & V. Shapiro. Ghosts in the nursery: A psychoanalytic approach to the problem of impaired infant-mother relationships. *Journal of the American Academy of Child Psychiatry, 14,* 3, 389.

one generation to the next. Lieberman, Padron and Harris expanded on this metaphor:

> The ghosts, representing the repetition of the past in the present, acquire corporeal form through punitive or neglectful caregiving practices. The parent fails to recognize the meaning of the child's signals of need, either ignoring or misconstruing them as evidence of the child's inherent badness and responding with anger and rejection. In these instances, the immediacy of the parent's visceral reaction takes precedence over the baby's developmental needs. As the recipient of the parent's negative attributions, the child progressively internalizes a sense of self unworthy and undeserving of love that can derail the course of healthy development."[33]

Inside Masha's mother, everything feels paralyzed and frozen, overgrown with severe defenses. Meanwhile, her youngest daughter is still fighting. She won't give up and is crying out her pain.

MOTHER: *How can I be sure that therapy will help me understand my child?*

I hear the mother say: what is the guarantee that I will not get hurt again, like when I was a child, when I come near the source of this childhood nightmare?

THERAPIST: *There are no guarantees unfortunately, but there is a possibility.*

And yes, in order to hear her, she has to hear herself. I often get stuck in a loop of desperation during parental consultations. Across generations, children who were frustrated by severe parenting grow up and start torturing their own young children.

The externally imposed system of raising "future builders of Communism" collapsed and was replaced by chaos. Now they say that

---

[33] A. Lieberman, E. Padron & W. W. Harris. Angels in the Nursery: The Intergenerational Transmission of Benevolent Parental Influences, *Infant Mental Health Journal, 26*, 6, 508.

we need new methods of birthing and parenting. For instance, they say we must breastfeed forever and let children share our beds. This will make them healthier and calmer. From one extreme, when a Soviet child was raised as a parentless ant, socially useful and ideologically rooted, we have jumped to the other extreme, when parents decline to prepare the child to enter the unsafe world outside the family.

Mothers share experiences of co-sleeping with the baby, which often involves moving the father into another room. We discuss teaching a child to do things independently, for example, take a bath or wipe their own bottom. We talk about feeding children according to their needs and letting them go out unsupervised. The child's real age doesn't always match the mother's fantasies.

The most devastating allegation made by Winnicott[34] against mothers who "do all the right things at the right moments" is that they do "something worse than castrate the infant." He goes on to say that two possibilities are open to the infant of such a mother: "either being in a permanent state of regression and of being merged with the mother, or else staging a total rejection of the mother, even of the seemingly good mother."[35]

Children find themselves locked inside their mother, with the rejected or abandoned inner child inside. The mother rescues them from dreadful nurseries, from bad neighborhood kids, and then from school. Normal healthy children get homeschooled, stuck home alone. The images we see in those children's drawings and sandplay are traps, prisons and cages.

A parental consultation can feel like acting as a midwife during the birth of a baby carried past the due date, when labor shows no sign of starting. We nurture the idea of separation and try to open the doors. However, the older the child, the further they are from the developmental stage of separation and individuation and the stronger they hold onto the door from the inside. Another little girl, six-year-old Vera, had this kind of problem. For the first several months of therapy, she fluttered about the room, running from the door to the window and back, asking where

---

[34] D. W. Winnicott, *The Maturational Processes and the Facilitating Environment*, 51.
[35] D. W. Winnicott, *The Maturational Processes and the Facilitating Environment*, 51.

her mother was and when she would return. In the countertransference, I felt life-and-death anxiety for this child.

Another example comes from the work with a teenage boy. At 14, Grisha gradually gave up all activity and interests, to the point where he even stopped playing with gadgets, spending most of his time lying on his back staring at the ceiling. His mother and father accompanied him to our first session. In the waiting room, the mother literally forced her adolescent son and husband to go to the toilet, telling them, "You need to go, you haven't gone for a while." At a separate session with the father, he told me that his wife owned all of them. The boy had no experience of traveling anywhere without his parents. He attended an art school that he hated and was waiting for it to be finally over, as he told me himself. Given that he had diabetes from a young age, it all sounded tragic.

One often hears that the father drinks; the father complex appears deficient or constellated in addictions. The mother complex, in its turn, can be controlling, endlessly nurturing and often restraining. We can probably consider our space a matriarchy in which the mother is the Hero and the man is her son and assistant. The family is therefore a matriarchal system where self-regulation is very different for men and women.

Children who are brought into therapy often live with their mothers, sometimes with a mother and a grandmother. In such families, fathers stay for a few years and then move on to other households. Britton writes:

> The primary family triangle provides the child with two links connecting him separately with each parent and confronts him with the link between them which excludes him ... If the link between the parents perceived in love and hate can be tolerated in the child's mind, it provides him with a prototype for an object relationship of a third kind in which he is a witness and not a participant. The third position then comes into existence from which object relationships can be observed. Given this, we can also envisage being observed. This provides us with a capacity for seeing ourselves in interaction with others and for entertaining another point of view whilst retaining our own, for reflecting on ourselves whilst being ourselves." [36]

---

[36] R. Britton, The Missing Link: Parental Sexuality in the Oedipus Complex. In J. Steiner (Ed.), *The Oedipus Complex Today,* 89.

An important part of the therapy is to return the father to the child, since mothers often think fathers are useless. We discuss the importance of a father for a child and the role he needs to play in a child's life. In such cases, when we invite the father, it often turns out that he is willing to be in touch with his child but cannot, for various reasons, sometimes because the mother prevents him. Sometimes it turns out that the father himself grew up without a father and has no idea how to communicate with his own child.

Of course, in many ways, we all, Russian therapists and patients surrounded by family members, are still surviving and just learning to live. Perhaps, Russian patience and faith are the spiritual components of the cultural complex, the part that prevents us from falling all the way into the abyss of despair. One of our Western teachers said that psychotherapy in Russia is trauma psychotherapy performed by traumatized people. Individual trauma is part of the shared cultural trauma, containing the trauma of the outside world.

We certainly need faith. We need to believe in the psyche's self-curing abilities and in what the Self can achieve. This is exactly what attracts us in Jung's ideas. He writes:

> As we know, a complex can be really overcome only if it is lived out to the full. In other words, if we are to develop further we have to draw to us and drink down to the very dregs what, because of our complexes, we have held at a distance.[37]

## On Therapy within the Russian Cultural Complex

Psychotherapy with children and adolescents allows the therapist to feel what it is like to be inside the child's skin or mind, to understand the young patient's mostly non-verbal narrative, to get connected to the child's or adolescent's inner infant, both under pressure of the family's projections and separate from them, and to help her or him to individuate. Very often, the therapist can feel deeply confused or even caught in a complicated transference. Our practices show, this transference contains the message of the collective trauma. By helping this message

---

[37] C.G. Jung. *CW 9i*, ¶ 184.

to be understood (initially received wholeheartedly by the therapist and thereby proved survivable), known to the child's conscious mind and grieved, traumas can be healed.

Angela Connolly thinks healing the child's trauma is impossible without "healing the wounds of our fathers."[38] In this process, it happens that transgenerational trauma brings up distant pieces of memory akin to non-specific flashbacks, unrooted in the nearest past, either in the child's or in the parents.' It feels that the thinner the personal layer of one's psyche, the thicker and denser is the psychic layer of the family's unconscious and the more powerful is the negative cultural complex's operation in that situation.

Such was the case with one of our adolescent patients. He will be called Vanya (short for Ivan) for our purposes. We met in 2003 after he was diagnosed with adolescent paranoid schizophrenia at the age of 12. His entrance into the consulting room, propped up and almost propelled by his mother, remains vivid in this author's memory. When he 'sank' into an armchair, his body hung over the arm as though he had no spine or bones within, no structure, a coat without a person within. I witnessed his slow walks-in and sinks-in for many more sessions. Not knowing whether I would be able to help him or not was frightening and heart-breaking. His limp body reminded me of the deposition from the cross. A transition from the child's real mother to the symbolic one for the purpose of re-birth was in action. Jung's phrase from his pivotal "Symbols of Transformation", namely 'Symbols of the mother and rebirth', helped me a lot: "The dead are delivered back to the mother for rebirth."[39]

From early childhood, Vanya was educated by both his parents, but mostly by his mother and grandmothers who lived in the countryside, to be responsive only to the concrete. They denigrated his emotional life by calling him weak or bad whenever he expressed his feelings. Scared of their own inner realms, they made him scared of making mistakes and showing his feelings, because these behaviors would have numerous negative consequences. The parents and grandmothers wanted their son

---

[38] A. Connolly. Healing the Wounds of our Fathers: Intergenerational Trauma, Memory, Symbolization and Narrative, *The Journal for Analytical Psychology*, 56, 5, 609.

[39] C.G. Jung. *CW 9i*, ¶ 1.

and grandson to grow manageable, obedient, and helpful. He was taught never to trust people beyond the family circle. He was not punished physically but was constantly intimidated. Any time Vanya tried to experiment with his "negative" feelings and get hold of his inner fire, i.e., master his aggression to be able to defend himself in various situations at school and home, he was bitterly reprimanded, shamed and told something bad would definitely happen to him. Vanya was taught the world was a dangerous place to step into, whereas his parental world was suffocating. He found himself stuck, both unable to find a place within the parental world or to leave it without their approval. Separation was desperately needed for Vanya to individuate, yet equally dreaded, since having anger was forbidden.

When puberty came, Vanya found himself first unable to follow his teacher's narration (fear of disintegration), and then permanently trapped in a mystical dread of the letter A. The therapy lasted for fifteen years and was a combination of multiple breakthroughs, setbacks, and two interruptions. However, we continued, and the stronger Vanya felt within, the mightier also seemed his deep, irrational, "mystical" fear of the letter 'A'. It is still hard to say what exactly the Indo-European 'Letter A' represented for Vanya, perhaps, many aspects of undiscovered novelty, including sexuality and aggression, the need to become autonomous, and possibly some of the family's inter- or transgenerational trauma "incarnated" in the child's mind. However, the more openly he was able to talk about his inner life, the more he could reflect on his states of mind and observe them, especially his terrible persecution anxiety. Paradoxically for Vanya and rather predictable if looked at from the needs of the family system homeostasis, his mother, who initiated and supported the therapy for the first four years, later on became its strong critic. Vanya's growing self-assertion was moving him out of the "scapegoat" status in the family.

When he was 18, it became easier for Vanya to blame his parents' fears for his "rabbit character." He once called himself a coward which made it easier to verbalize his aim – to become a hero, the one who dares to speak and act from one's truth. Yet, it still was incredibly difficult for him to accept his full-on aggression, as well as to believe he would be loved while being aggressive towards the therapist who was blamed for not helping enough. Deep inside, he still believed his hate could not be "pardoned," i.e., tolerated and understood as meaningful. He was still longing for a "rebirth" and yet horrified by the inevitability of unimaginable punishment he would have to go through if his aggression might reveal itself. This dread made him loyal to his intimidating inner parents. I suggested we could think together on his inner deep anticipation of some punishment for in my mind he had gone through every possible psychic pain that damaged him for having done nothing wrong.

Then one day external events added up to bring out the fire in Vanya's inner world. The idea of punishment for any 'liberty' was linked to the family's history of being peasants under serfdom before 1917 and then Soviet collective farmers, without passports and salaries, almost until the late 1960s, i.e., with very few individual rights and freedoms. Vanya's parents were the first generation who had the willpower to move to the city and be educated in other than peasants' skills. Yet, every summer as a young child and later as a schoolboy for his summer vacation, Vanya would stay in the countryside with his grandparents, who were full of superstitions and most incredible fears, while never alluding directly to their true past histories, teeming with emotional and physical bullying.

All those fears and deep-down anxieties were gradually revealed within the therapeutic container. Yet, almost until he was 25, Vanya continued to be scared of his spontaneity and passion. One day his rage suddenly emerged, triggered by the conflict between Russia and Ukraine which started soon after the Russian annexation of Crimea in 2014. He let himself side with the aggressive position and for the first time I witnessed Vanya, then 25, talk freely without controlling his hate and expressing the fiery wish to fight and be ready to kill and die. He shared powerful images that made me shudder within. And then, unexpectedly both for me and evidently for himself, he yelled in the air: "And what a nice red rooster we gave them!"

Despite the horror I experienced within, I stayed present for Vanya, helping him think and confront the bitter truth. While listening to Vanya's first and powerful outburst of raw rage, a true revolt of the oppressed, I thought of the huge amounts of unprocessed pain not only in Vanya, but also in his parents and in his distant ancestors. When the "eruption" was nearing its end, a wave of guilt and shame filled up the container, my body and my mind. I said to Vanya that his psyche had just accomplished a huge task. It found the images for the rage, the rage of 'A' quality, the truth he was scared of for a long time. Yet, the peasants who set their proprietors' mansions on fire, I continued, acted out of retaliation because they could not express their suffering mentally and verbally. There was no one to hear them mindfully. Acting out rage brings guilt and shame. We needed to put an end to the vicious circle of anger-guilt-shame, to helplessness. I wanted Vanya to feel the difference between his emotions, images and words, on the one hand, and acting out; that we were together to talk, feel and think about his deepest emotions and, by doing this, to process them and let the past become the past.

Although generally it was clear what was meant by the "red rooster," I asked Vanya to expand on that image. A deeply troubling family story came out. In Russia before the abolishment of serfdom in 1861, setting a landlord's house on fire--"sending the red rooster"--by the serfs who were owned by the landlord's family exactly as they owned farming tools, meant that the serfs' limit to tolerate pain, psychic and physical, had been reached. This act of hate was similar to a suicide, yet, in their thinking, by maximally destroying the possessions of the oppressor and hopefully, the oppressors themselves, they honored and exacted justice, the only way they could. The red rooster, a fire god, was associated with both destructive flames and a new dawn (new birth, or re-birth) in Slavic tribes.

Like many parents, Vanya's parents used him as a container for them-selves and the family unconscious with its traumatic complex. It took the therapy fifteen years for the child's mind to grow and differentiate from the stories of his parents and ancestors.

## Conclusion

Many Russian analysts live and work in Moscow, St. Petersburg and other big cities where the level of consciousness grows faster compared to the numerous smaller cities and towns in Russia, due to much greater educational opportunities and better living conditions. Internationally established educational networks and fast internet also provide us, living in big cities, with learning opportunities and access to new understandings and breakthroughs in the study of the psyche.

We are deeply grateful to our supervisors and tutors from the International Association of Analytical Psychology (IAAP) and the International Society for Sandplay Therapy (ISST) who gave us the best they have—Murray Stein and Gert Zauer, Penny Pickles and Cathy Kaplinsky, Martin Stone and Moira Duckworth, Jan Wiener and Catherine Crowther, Susanne Short and Angela Connolly, Martin Schmidt and Alex Esterhuyzen, Anne Webster and Lucy Hammond, Alessandra Cavalli and Brian Feldman, Marica Rytovaara, Carlo Ruffino, Ulrike Hinsch, and Elvira Valente, just to name a few.

Infant observation seminars organized by Brian Feldman (starting in 2013) and the training course on child psychoanalysis bridging the gap between Kleinian and Jungian theories, prepared and implemented by Alessandra Cavalli (2014-2020) are important cornerstones in the edifice laid by the IAAP training analysts to further the analytical education of Russian analysts. Infant observation seminars run by Feldman and the Cavallian training course based on the Tavistock model for child analysts run weekly and monthly over the years have helped us to know more and more deeply how to be available to the child as a good enough four-functioning *quarternio* in the clinical practice, satisfying the 'need' to know (infant's function), 'supply' (maternal function), wish for 'limitations' (paternal function) and 'observation' (being firm and calm while observing as an empathic mind, independent of the previous three functions and roles).[40] Infant observation and clinical supervision also allowed us 'to witness' how the transmission of cultural traumas takes place in infancy and even in utero.

These experiences gave us a deeper and broader understanding of the vicissitudes of individuation after the conception and development of the child's mind in utero and postnatally, as well as the hardships an infant undergoes to become a truly human child in a very complicated

---

[40] A. Cavalli. The Relevance of the Concept of the Quarternio to Clinical Practice, Unpublished manuscript, 2019.

and ever-changing triadic interaction, our common human home, 'programmed' by a major 'psychic factor' which Jung named archetype.

All this and the sensitively shared observations and reflections of our Western teachers and colleagues who individuated in different cultural complexes with different traumas helped us to recognize the unique elements and highs and lows of our Russian cultural complex, the immediate basis for both Russian patients and therapists. Some of the many difficult and hard-to-reach areas of the Russian cultural complex have become open to observation and self-study within the recent busy decades. This observation and self-study promotes our working psychoanalytically with children and adolescents, as well as with their parents, although, now and then, psychotherapy seems akin to the labors of Sisyphus. Albert Camus comes to help:

> Sisyphus, proletarian of the gods, powerless and rebellious, knows the whole extent of his wretched condition: it is what he thinks of during his descent. The lucidity that was to constitute his torture at the same time crowns his victory... If the descent is thus sometimes performed in sorrow, it can also take place in joy. The struggle itself towards the heights is enough to fill a man's heart."[41]

Il faut imaginer Sisyphus heureux.[42] ["You must imagine that Sisyphus is happy."]

> I yearn to live a life of meaning:
> Make every sheer thing – immortalized,
> Make all the formal – humanized,
> Bring non-existent – into being![43]

---

[41] A. Camus, *The Myth of Sisyphus and Other Essays*.

[42] A. Camus, *The Myth of Sisyphus and Other Essays*.

[43] A. Blok, I Yearn to Live a Life of Meaning.

# REFERENCES

Alexiyevich, S. On the Battle Lost. *The Nobel Prize Speech, 2015,* accessed from *www.nobelprize.org*

Blok, A. *I yearn to live a life of meaning...* Originally published 1914. In Russian at the Internet Portal of Open Data of the Ministry of Culture of the Russian Federation (2004-2020), 1914. English translation by A. Kneller. https://nonbookreviews.wordpress.com/2016/02/28/ the-stranger-selected-poetry-alexander-blok-andrey-kneller-translator

Britton, R. The Missing Link: Parental sexuality in the Oedipus complex. In Steiner, J. (Ed.), *The Oedipus Complex Today*, London, UK: Karnac, 83-101, 1989.

Brodsky, J. *Letters to a Roman Friend (after Martial).* In Russian, Internet Portal of Open Data of the Ministry of Culture in Russian Federation, 1972, www. opendata.mkrf.ru

Bulgakov, M. *The Heart of the Dog.* First Published, 1925. (A. Pyram, Trans.). Moscow, Russia: Raduga Publishers, 1990.

Camus, A. *The Myth of Sisyphus and Other Essays*. Published in French, 1942. First publication in English, (J. O'Brien, Trans.). Knopf: New York, NY, 1955. Reprinted by Vintage Press: New York, NY, 1991. Kindle Edition.

Cavalli, A. Transgenerational Transmission of Indigestible Facts: from Trauma, Deadly Ghosts and Mental Voids to Meaning-Making Interpretations. *The Journal of Analytical Psychology, 57,* 5, 597-614, 2012.

Cavalli, A. The Relevance of the Concept of the Quaternio to Clinical Practice. Unpublished manuscript shared with author, 2019.

—— Moscow Seminar, September 13, 2014.

Chudakova, M. Interview with journalist L. Velechov on Radio Svoboda (Freedom). June 27, 2015, www.radiosvoboda.ru

Chukovskaya, L. *Notes on Anna Akhmatova. Vol. 2, 1952-1962*, Moscow, Russia, 1997, 41. [In Russian.]

Connolly, A. Healing the Wounds of our Fathers: Intergenerational Trauma, Memory, Symbolization and Narrative. *The Journal for Analytical Psychology, 56,* 5, 607-626, 2011.

Dostoyevsky, F. *Humiliated and Insulted.* (I. Avsey, Trans.). St. Petersburg, Russia: Alma Classics, 2018. (First published in Journal *'Vremya'*, Saint Petersburg, Russian Empire, 1861.

Fainalova, E. Political anecdote from 1934, quoted in podcast: From Lenin to Putin, Radio Svoboda (In Russian), 2020. https://www.svoboda.org/a/30352863.html

Feldman, B. The Cultural Skin in China. In *Research in Analytical Psychology*: *Empirical Research, 1st Edition*. (C. Roesler, Ed.) London, UK: Karnac Books, 2018.

——Comment made during the online seminar on infant observation, March 20, 2018.

Fonvizin, D. *Brigadier-General.* Act 3, Scene 1. Internet Library of Alexey Komarov, 1769. [In Russian.] https://ilibrary.ru/text/1643/1/index.html

Fraiberg, S., Adelson, E., & Shapiro, V. Ghosts in the nursery: A psychoanalytic approach to the problem of impaired infant-mother relationships. *Journal of the American Academy of Child Psychiatry, 14,* 3, 387-421, 1975.

Gordon, R. *Bridges. Metaphor for Psychic Processes,* London, UK: Karnac Books, 1993.

Griboyedov, A. *Woe from Wit, Act 1, Scene 2,* 1823. (A. S. Vagapov, Trans., 1993), accessed from vladivostok.com/speaking_in_tongues/griboyedov.htm

Henderson, J. *Cultural Attitudes in Psychological Perspective.* Toronto, Canada: Inner City Books, 1984.

*Internationale,* written in French by Eugène Pottier, 1871. First Russian version, 1902 by Arkady Kots. Modified by Communist leaders after the Bolshevik Revolution and by the USSR government. USSR national anthem, 1918-1944. https://en.wikipedia.org/wiki/The_Internationale

Ivanov, V. The Lord Sleeps Between the Lines. Moscow. AST: CORPUS, 2019. [In Russian.]

Jung, C.G. *The Collected Works, Second Edition.* (Bollingen Series XX; H Read, M. Fordham, & G. Adler, Eds.; R.C.F. Hull, Trans.). Princeton, NJ: Princeton University Press, 1953-1979.

——Archetypes of the Collective Unconscious. *The Archetypes and the Collective Unconscious, The Collected Works, Vol. 9i,* 1934/1954.

——Psychological Aspects of the Mother Complex. *The Archetypes and the Collective Unconscious, The Collected Works, Vol. 9i,* 1938/1954.

——Symbols of the Mother and Rebirth. *Symbols of Transformation, The Collected Works, Vol. 5,* 1911-12/1952.

Lieberman, A., Padron, E. and W.W. Harris. Angels in the nursery: The intergenerational transmission of benevolent parental influences. *Infant Mental Health Journal, 26,* 6, 504-520, 2005.

Lotman, Y. Russian Literature of the Post-Petrine Era and the Christian Tradition. In *Yu.M. Lotman and the Tartu-Moscow Semiotic School.* Gnosis, 1994. [In Russian.]

Martynov, V. *Motley Twigs of Jacob: On the End of the Time of Russian Literature.* Moscow, Russia: Modern Russian Philosophy, 2009. [In Russian.]

Merriam-Webster Online Dictionary. www.merriam-webster.com

Morgan, H. Exploring Racism, *Journal of Analytical Psychology, 47,* 4. 567-581, 2002.

Nekrasov, N. Who Is Happy in Russia? www.library.ru. Internet Library of Alexei Komarov. Collected Works, Vol. 5. Written 1866-1879. Published 1982, Nauka Press: Moscow, Russia

Radzinsky, E. *Stalin: The First In-Depth Biography Based on Explosive New Documents from Russia's Secret Archives.* New York, NY: Knopf-Doubleday, 1997.

——Interview on January 3, 2009 at *echo.msk.ru.* [In Russian.]

——Why Ancharov? In G. Schekina *The Collection of Essays, Vol. 6.* Moscow, Russia & Berlin, Germany: Direkt-Media, 2020.

Singer, T. The Cultural Complex and Archetypal Defenses of the Group Spirit: Baby Zeus, Elian Gonzales, Constantine's Sword, and other Holy Wars. In *The Cultural Complex: Contemporary Jungian Perspectives on Psyche and Society.* (Singer T. and Kimbels, S., Eds.) London, UK: Brunner-Routledge, 13-35, 2004.

——The Cultural Complex and Archetypal Defenses of the Collective Spirit, *The San Francisco Jung Institute Library Journal, 20,* 4, 5-28, 2002.

Solzhenitsyn, A. *One Day in the Life of Ivan Denisovich.* New York, NY: Bantam-Dell, 1962.

Tischler, S. Being with a Psychotic Child: A Psycho-Analytical Approach to the Problems of Parents of Psychotic Children. *International Journal of Psycho-Analysis, 60,* p 29-38, 1979.

Tolstoy, L. *War and Peace,* Published 1869/2019. English version (L. & A. Maude Trans.) at www.guttenberg.org

Waddell, M. *Inside Lives: Psychoanalysis and the Growth of the Personality.* London, UK: Karnac Books Ltd., 2002.

Winnicott, D.W. *The Maturational Processes and the Facilitating Environment.* London, UK: Routledge, 1990.

Yudin, G. Who are we – Individualists or Collectivists? Lecture reprinted in *Smart Power Journal,* December 6, 2018.

Zauer, G. Lecture at the First European Conference of Analytical Psychology, September 5-7, 2008, Vilnius

Zoja, L. *The Cultural Complex: Contemporary Jungian Perspectives on Psyche and Society.* London, UK: Brunner-Routledge, 2004.

# ACKNOWLEDGMENTS

ABOVE ALL, I WANT to thank the Jungian analysts from around the world who contributed to this book: Moshe Alon from Israel, Caterina Vezzoli from Italy, Lavinia Țânculescu-Popa from Romania, Mei-Fang Huang from Taiwan, Batya Brosh Palmoni who spoke on the Kibbutz experience from Israel, Lucia Azevedo from Brazil, and Elena Bortuleva and Viktoria Andreeva from Russia. I am grateful for their heartfelt dedication and commitment to this project. In addition, I want to express my sorrow that Alessandra Cavalli, who was excited about this project, was prevented by her untimely death from sharing her wisdom in these pages.

The verbal fluency of this book has benefitted greatly from the copy-editing of Elizabeth H. Maury, a friend and fellow clinical psychologist. Fortunately for me, she loves doing this kind of work. I am most grateful!

The funding for this book came in part from the Scholarship Committee at the C.G. Jung Institute-San Francisco. I want to thank Susan Bostrom-Wong, Chair, Margo Leahy and Steven Joseph for their interest and support.

I extend gratitude to Dyane Sherwood for having the vision and for her support to see this book to publication and Mel Mathews, publisher of Fisher King Press, who supported the inspiration for this book.

Audrey Punnett
Fresno, California, USA

# INDEX

## A

adolescence  38, 48, 50, 61, 134, 136, 141, 160

adolescent  1–3, 5–7, 9, 11–13, 15, 17, 19, 21, 23, 25, 27–28, 48–49, 59–60, 64, 109, 122–125, 133–134, 136–137, 141, 144, 153, 173, 176–177, 185, 195, 197–198, 203, 219–221

African-American  52–55, 61, 161

aggression  48, 58, 75, 90, 93, 99, 101, 103–108, 111, 199–200

analytical therapy  16, 136

anxiety  10, 13, 24, 42, 69–71, 96, 116–117, 130–131, 161–162, 167–168, 192, 195, 199–200

automorphism  136–137, 148

## B

Brazilian culture  154

## C

C.G. Jung Institute of Los Angeles  60

C.G. Jung Institute of San Francisco, 58, 221

centroversion  136–137, 144

child  1–50, 52, 54, 56–74, 76, 78, 80–81, 83–111, 113–140, 142–146, 148–178, 180, 182–203, 205–206, 219–222

child analysis  1–2, 4, 6, 8, 10, 12, 14, 16–18, 20, 22, 24, 26, 28–50, 52, 54, 56, 58–60, 62, 64, 66, 68, 70, 72, 74, 76, 78, 80, 84, 86, 88, 90, 92, 94, 96, 98, 100, 102, 104, 106–108, 110, 113–132, 134, 136, 138, 140, 142, 144, 146, 148, 150, 152–174, 176, 178, 180, 182, 184, 186, 188, 190, 192, 194, 196, 198, 200, 202, 206, 220–222

child and adolescent psychotherapy  13, 124

child care  63–64, 80–81

child therapy, 16, 33, 44, 153, 168, 174

child training  36, 59

Chinese culture  115, 122, 131

civil rights  53–56

Civil War, 53, 115, 183, 186, 188

collective consciousness  155–156, 158, 173

collective education  135, 137

collective trauma  83–85, 87, 89, 91, 93, 95, 97, 99, 101, 103, 105, 107–109, 111, 177, 188, 197

## AUTHOR BIOGRAPHIES

**Moshe Alon**, M.A., is a Jungian Analyst, licensed Educational Psychologist-Supervisor and family therapist. He is past President of the New Israeli Jungian Association (NIJA) and teaches and supervises in its training program. He is former head of educational/psychological services in Tel-Aviv-Jaffa. He now works in Lod as a supervisor in educational/psychological services. Lod has a mixed population of Jews, Arabs, and new Jewish immigrants from Ethiopia and the former U.S.S.R., foreign workers, and refugee seekers. His clinic treats children, adolescents, and adults. He has expertise with trauma, including sexual abuse and crisis intervention. He has published papers on transference, countertransference and the wounded healer, and trauma and psychotherapy with children. He presented at the 2016 Twentieth International Congress on Analytical Psychology in Kyoto, the 2019 First Analytical Psychology Conference on Children and Adolescents, Moscow, and the 2020 Conference on Analysis and Activism, Berkeley, California.

**Viktoria Andreeva**, M.A., is a Jungian analyst and supervisor for the International Association for Analytical Psychology (IAAP) and the Russian Society for Analytical Psychology (RSAP). She is a Tavistock model-based child psychotherapist and sandplay therapist (Teaching Member of the International Society for Sandplay Therapy--TM/ISST) in private practice with children and adults in Moscow. She organized the First and Second Russian Conferences on Sandplay Therapy in 2020 and 2021. She has contributed articles to the Russian Journal of Jungian Analysis (Moscow). She contributed to and edited the proceedings of the Moscow Sandplay Therapy Conference, 2021. She teaches sandplay therapy and supervises sandplay cases in Moscow.

**Lucia Azevedo**, M.S., Licensed Psychologist, is a Child and Adult Jungian Analyst in private practice in Sao Paulo, Brazil. She is an analyst member of the Brazilian Society for Analytical Psychology (SBrPA), where she was a former board member and editor of the Junguiana, SBrPA Journal. She was also a teacher and supervisor in the trainee program. She is a member of the International Association for Analytical Psychology (IAAP). She is a Teaching Member and President of the Brazilian Institute for Sandplay Therapy (IBTSandplay), and Teaching Member in the International Society for Sandplay Therapy (ISST). She has published articles in Jungian journals and contributed book chapters on the treatment of children and families, the importance of the image in individuation, and other topics. She has presented her work at several international congresses.

**Elena Bortuleva**, M.A. is a clinical psychologist, adult Jungian Analyst and supervisor (IAAP/RSAP), and Tavistock model-based child psychotherapist. She sees children, adolescents and adults in her private practice in Moscow and Prague. She has worked as a family and couples' therapist and psychoanalytic teacher in Tula, Moscow, St. Petersburg, Krasnodar, Voronezh and Vladivostok, Russia, Riga, Latvia, and Prague, Czechia. She has contributed articles to the Russian Journal of Jungian Analysis (Moscow) and the Journal of Analytical Psychology (JAP, 2014). She was an organizer of the First International Jungian Child and Adolescent Conference in Moscow, April 2019.

**Batya Brosh Palmoni**, M.A., is President of the Israel Institute of Jungian Psychology (IIJP), and a Senior Jungian Analyst, training analyst and supervisor. For over thirty years she worked as a psychologist in a public mental health clinic run by the Kibbutz movement, while also having a private analytical practice. She is a Lecturer at Bar Ilan University in the program of Jungian Psychotherapy. Between 2013-2019, she served on the Executive Committee of IAAP in the Child and Adolescent Working Group, facilitating the First International Jungian Child and Adolescent Conference in Moscow, Russia. For the past ten years, she has acted as supervisor, lecturer, and liaison person for the Developing Group of Kiev, Ukraine. Her work there has expanded her understanding of the great contribution of Jung and Neumann for clinicians living far from the traditional centers of analytical psychology.

**Mei-Fang Huang,** M.A., is a Licensed Counseling Psychologist. She is a Jungian Analyst and Secretary-General of the Taiwan Society of Analytical Psychology (TSAP) of the IAAP. She is an Adjunct Lecturer at Soochow University in Taipei, Taiwan. Her interests include fairy tales, Chinese folk tales and sandplay. She is one of the translators for the books, *Transformation: Emergence of the Self* by Murray Stein published by A & M University Press, and *Contemporary Man Still in Search of a Soul* by Thomas Kirsch (Chinese Version only), both published by PsyGarden Publishing Company. Ms. Huang has a private practice in Taipei, Taiwan.

**Audrey Punnett,** Ph.D., is a graduate of the C.G. Jung Institute, Zurich, with diplomas in both Child/Adolescent and Adult Analytical Psychology. She is a member of the Association of Graduate Analytical Psychologists (AGAP) and the C.G. Jung Institute of San Francisco (CGJSFI). Dr. Punnett is Associate Clinical Professor of Psychiatry, University of California San Francisco-Fresno; a Registered Play Therapist/Supervisor and Certified Sandplay Therapist/Teacher ISST. She is past president of the Board of Trustees, Sandplay Therapists of America and current Vice-President of the Americas/ISST. She has lectured and given work-shops in many countries. She has published in peer-reviewed journals and contributed chapters to: *The Handbook of Play Therapy, 2ⁿᵈ Edition* (2016), *Play Therapy with Preteens* (2018), and *Into the Heart of Sandplay* (2018). She is the author of *The Orphan: A Journey to Wholeness* (2014) and editor of *Jungian Child Analysis* (2018). Dr. Punnett maintains a private practice in Fresno, California.

**Lavinia Ţânculescu-Popa,** Ph.D., is one of the first six IAAP Jungian Analysts in Romania, officially entering the association at the IAAP Kyoto Conference in 2016, working with both children and adults since 2006. She is a member of AGAP (Switzerland) and of SRAJ and ARPA (Romania). She was the main translator for the *Handbook of Analytical Psychology*, edited by R. Papadopoulos, into Romanian. She is now working on a book of interviews with senior analysts, called *Beyond Persona with Jungian Analysts: Interviews on Individuation and Beginnings*, due to be published in 2022 by Routledge, UK. Dr. Țânculescu-Popa teaches at a private University in Bucharest and has academic collaborations with two other universities in Romania. Her research interests are in the areas of psychological anthropology, psychology and religion, and the unfolding of the Self in both the personal and organizational life of the individual in various cultural settings.

**Caterina Vezzoli**, Ph.D., Psychologist and Jungian Analyst, is a member of the Centro Italiano Psicologia Analitica (CIPA), the Associazione di Psicoterapia Psicoanalitica di Gruppo (APG) and IAAP. She is a training analyst for CIPA and the C.G. Jung Institute-Zurich. She was a visiting supervisor in Tunisia and Liaison Person for the Malta Developing Group. Dr. Vezzoli has published numerous papers in peer-reviewed journals, including articles in the *Journal of Analytical Psychology* and the *Jung Journal*, and has published in Europe *Many Souls* (2016), and *ARAS Connections: Image and Archetype* (2109); she edited *Jung Today* (2009) with Francesco Bisagni and Nadia Fina. Dr Vezzoli has contributed to the textbook, *Manuale di Psichiatria e Psicologia Clinica* (2017). Her research interests include gender studies, women in history, feminine mysticism, transference/countertransference, and psychological issues related to the COVID-19 pandemic, which have been recently published (2021). She maintains a private practice in Milan, Italy.

FRONT COVER AND ABOVE: Rufino Tamayo, *Children's Games*, 1959